The Sound of the Week

by Sally Barrett

illustrated by Mary Barton Wilson

Cover by Tom Sjoerdsma

Copyright © Good Apple, Inc., 1990 Revised

ISBN No. 0-916456-63-3

Printing No. 10

Good Apple, Inc.
1204 Buchanan St., Box 299
Carthage, IL 62321-0299

Preface

Two objectives in kindergarten classes today are for students to learn to recognize the letters of the alphabet and to know the sound that each represents. Since mastery of these skills is part of the basic foundation for reading, it is important that students achieve these objectives.

The Sound of the Week system has been developed in my kindergarten classes over a period of several years. Students have been successful in accomplishing the above objectives in an informal, varied, yet intentional and ordered manner that is integrated into all areas of the kindergarten program. These meaningful activities are directly related to the lives and experiences of the children, with the results being self-motivation and positive transfer. This program can also be adopted for first grade pupils who have not yet learned the letters and sounds and also for special education classes whose students are ready to move on to the printed page.

An important element in the success of this system is parental involvement. This is accomplished through various parent-teacher communications and through parental participation in providing snacks and items to share and also in serving as resource people.

Through the use of *The Sound of the Week* program, nonreaders will be given a comprehensive reading readiness program based on a full school week to learn each consonant and long vowel sound. At the same time they will acquire a foundation for structured learning through the development of essential skills such as listening, thinking, and following required directions to complete a task.

The Sound of the Week system is intended to be an open-ended and non-sequential program. All who use it are encouraged to augment, adapt, supplement, and vary it to meet the needs of their individual classes. Not all of the activities will be used in the classroom. This system is meant to provide resources that will enable the user to teach the letters and sounds in any geographical location, climate, or classroom arrangement. The program also allows for differences in class size, group dynamics, and teacher interest.

I am grateful to my parents, my fellow teachers and administrators and my family for their support and encouragement. They have all contributed to the development of an organized, useable, and exciting teacher-learner system.

It is hoped that this program will be an inspiration to you and your classes. And that it will be a positive learning experience for your students. Recognition of alphabet sounds and letters provides an important foundation for future learning. Good luck in your endeavors.

Best wishes,

Sally Barrett

GA184

Table of Contents

GA184

 # Introduction

The Concept

The Sound of the Week system is an instructional resource for teachers and parents of pre-readers. The program will facilitate the learning of consonant and long vowel sounds in a series of one week units based on inexpensive and readily available or simply-made materials.

When to Start

The program can begin at any time; however, experience has shown that the fall of the year is a period of orientation to the new classroom environment, a time for further readiness and development, and a time filled with the excitement of holidays, special days and other interests. Therefore it is recommended that *The Sound of the Week* program be started immediately following the December holidays. In the case of a year-round plan, it should begin near the beginning of the second quarter of school.

Suggested Sequence

The units are independent. They may be dealt with in any order. In this book they are described in a sequence that fits into the school year with consideration for seasonal change, important dates, and ease of mastery of particular letter sounds. Each year the sequence needs to be reviewed and each sound scheduled into the most appropriate week.

Kindergartners seem to be able to handle the material on a week-to-week basis. If, however, more than one week seems appropriate, there is no reason why the teacher cannot lengthen the unit.

Many of the less frequently used letters do not demand a full week of attention. Later in the year, they can be dealt with in just a day or two. Confusion seems to result if more than one letter is dealt with at one time.

2

GA184

Constants in the Classroom Environment

The constants in this program are activities or interest centers that are used for every letter-sound developed. Although they require change to the new letter every week, their constancy serves as a familiar friend and confidence builder as the children approach the learning of each new individual sound.

Sounds Bulletin Board

The sounds bulletin board is any standard bulletin board in the room that is easily accessible to the children. It is used to display pictures and objects as well as examples of the letter-sound being presented. The children are encouraged to bring, share and post by themselves items for this bulletin board. Since the board is always changing, it should be simply arranged.

A collection of either upper or lower-case letters from magazines and newspapers or manufactured and teacher-made letters is essential. Several sizes and samples of the letter for the week should be placed on the board. Letters can also be found or made from interesting materials such as wood, plastic, fabric or metal.

The Word-Object Table

The word-object table is a place to display items that can't be accommodated on a bulletin board. Each week several objects starting with *The Sound of the Week* are placed on the table. Early in the program the objects may be traced and the tracings labeled with their word names. The children can then match objects to the labeled tracings. Later in the program, simple label cards can be made to accompany the objects. If there is a color that starts with *The Sound of the Week* letter, make labels using that color or write them with that color pen or crayon. The children should match the object to the word label. The tracing is a helpful clue in the early weeks. As the children learn more sounds and learn clues such as "longer words contain more letters," the labels will make them think more independently and prevent them from matching shapes without using the sound clues. Much later, unmatched labels or objects may be included to further challenge thinking skills.

GA184

Monograms

Monograms are cutouts of the letter for the week. On Monday of each week a number of monograms should be available. If there is a color word that starts with the letter of the week, that color is used to make the monograms. While taking attendance or as the children arrive, supply each child who has the letter for an initial with a monogram to wear. Monograms can also be presented to teachers, the librarian, the nurse, the custodian or classroom pets, or attached to objects in the room whenever appropriate.

Mobile

As each week begins, a mobile sign hanging in a prominent place in the room (such as near the door) can be updated so that it tells all who pass by what the sound is for the week. When others are informed, they frequently drop in to contribute an item of interest. When they meet the children in the halls, they often greet them with sound words or strike up conversations that relate to the sound or elicit from the children words of response using the week's sound.

Magic Box

Any large box with a lid can become the Magic Box. It is painted or covered in some attractive way. To start off *The Sound of the Week* program, small, interesting objects or treats are placed in the box for the children to identify by guessing from clues and by asking questions. The children are asked to bring objects to contribute to the box which will help develop thinking and questioning skills and will also relate to *The Sound of the Week*.

Continuing Tests

There are several manufactured alphabet-sound games relating to learning sounds that should be available to the children for interest center practice. Teachers can also make simple progress tests. An example would be "Track the Monster." The teacher prepares large footprints for each letter. As each sound is taught, that print is attached to a wall or even to the floor. The children "track the monster" by identifying the letter and giving a word that starts with its sound. By correctly naming the letter on each footprint, they reach the monster (a drawing or stuffed toy) and sign their names on it.

A badge system is helpful as motivation and serves to test the system in several ways. A badge can be given for identifying all the upper-case letters, one for identification of the lower-case letters, another for giving words to match the sound and another for picking out the letters alphabetically from the out-of-sequence order in which they were presented. The easiest task, the identification

GA184

of the upper-case letters, is on the bottom and is clipped off and awarded when the skill is mastered. The rest of the badges are awarded the same way.

Equipment

Among the permanent pieces of classroom equipment that can be used in *The Sound of the Week* program are flannel boards, magnetic boards, alphabet cards, matching cards, dice and card games, Lotto and Bingo with letters and sounds, puzzles, and Wipe Off Cards (available from Trend Enterprises, St. Paul, Minnesota).

It is also helpful to have available picture files and old catalogs for cutting out sound pictures.

Library materials such as books, prints and film catalogs are resources that could be scheduled to fit the sounds. These are provided with each section. Copies of beginning picture dictionaries are invaluable.

Songs

In the repertoire of the kindergarten classroom, there are several songs that lend themselves to variations by changing the words. Two such songs are "The Bear Went Over the Mountain" and "Nice Little Dog." These songs can be easily changed to fit the section being studied. Name an animal that has *The Sound of the Week* letter for its beginning letter and use it in the song. A few examples that can be used are alligator for "A" week, cat or cougar for "C" week and turtle for "T" week.

Snacks

Having foods that accompany *The Sound of the Week* is one of the best ways to reinforce the sound concept. The social celebration aspect combined with the benefits of good nutrition and refreshments will help more children remember the letter and its sound.

This concept sounds like a huge project, but in reality it need not be. First of all, parents can be informed either at a group meeting or by a letter similar to the following one:

Dear Parents,

We have decided to take a "straw poll" of this year's parents to see if we should implement a snack program for the purpose of providing a refreshing, nutritious, mid-morning pick-me-up. This refreshment would relate to *The Sound of the Week* program.

If the consensus favors this idea, it would mean that each family would need to provide a snack or the ingredients for making one at school. Snack suggestions will be provided by the teacher; each family would be responsible for providing a snack approximately five or six times for the remainder of the year. The idea would be to keep the snacks as simple and inexpensive as possible.

Please fill out the bottom form and return it to school this week.

Sincerely,
The Kindergarten Teachers

_____

_____ I would be willing to provide a snack suggested by the teacher five or six times this year.

_____ I do not wish to participate in a snack program.

Signed _____

If the response is good, the program is on its way. Each new group of parents needs to accept the concept and be willing to assume the responsibility for providing snacks to fit the sounds. If not, there are several alternatives discussed at the end of this section.

Assuming that the response is positive, foods need to be selected for preparing and serving. Include a few of the unusual ones to broaden the children's tastes. Nutrition is another consideration in the selection of the foods. Even though the so-called "snack" or "junk" foods are usually the easiest to serve, at least some recognition should be given to food value.

Another factor is the expense of snacks. Each new group of parents needs to accept the concept and be willing to assume the responsibility for providing snacks to fit the sounds. Once they have agreed to participate, parents should be urged to keep the snacks as simple and as inexpensive as possible. The main idea is stimulation for learning the sound, not filling the child's stomach. For example, half is probably plenty when serving snacks such as hot dogs or oranges.

6

GA184

Whenever possible the foods should be prepared and even grown in the classroom. This cannot always be done, so setting up assignments for parents will be another task. An attempt should be made to balance the cost. If a parent provides a relatively expensive snack one time, arrangements should be made so that he/she provides a less expensive one the next time. Preparation time is another consideration. If time is a factor for different parents, perhaps it is better to ask them to send ready-to-eat foods instead of those that require more preparation. It is also good to be aware of the kinds of households from which the children come. If sanitary conditions are less than desireable, that family can be asked to send items purchased in cans or boxes that need not be opened until they arrive at school. Because of the concern for disease, many schools prohibit the serving of home-baked goods at school. This factor must be checked before finalizing any selection list.

Using a form similar to the one below will allow assignments to be sent home several days in advance so that the parents can prepare the food or have time to shop.

Dear Mrs. _____,

The idea of serving a snack to accompany *The Sound of the Week* was overwhelmingly accepted, so we will ask you to send __(item)__ for _____(#)_____ on _____(date)_____.

Keep the snack as simple and inexpensive as possible. We appreciate your willingness to participate.

The Kindergarten Teachers

A nice follow-through gesture on the part of the children is to thank the parents for their contributions to the program. For instance, when fresh watermelon is sent out-of-season, a simple cutout of a melon or a poster saying "Watermelon Was Wonderful" makes a nice thank you. Stick to *The Sound of the Week* wherever possible. The children then sign the thank you, which is taken home by the host child.

The snack program can be carried out with a minimum of equipment, providing the teacher is able to bring her own equipment from home once in a while. The minimum items needed are:

hand can opener	9″ × 12″ pan
bottle opener	large bowl (plastic or stainless steel)
sharp knife	2 quart plastic decanter for pouring
large spoon	pot holder

For Serving:

    *plastic or disposable "old fashioned" glasses for use as cups or bowls
    *plastic spoons
     Strofoam meat trays
     napkins

*Can be taken home by teacher and washed for re-use.

Nice But Not Necessary:

hot plate	8 quart kettle
oven	wooden spoon for mixing
tea kettle	measuring spoons
sauce pans	measuring cups
scouring pads	detergent
scrubber	dish towel and cloth

There are several alternatives to daily snacks provided by parents. The teacher might estimate the total cost and divide it among the class members. Snacks might be served only once or twice a week either as an introductory motivator or as a culminating activity. Since this program is less expensive than many published series, perhaps the district will budget the snack program as a language arts item. There have been grants awarded for classroom cooking programs. This possibility is worth investigating.

Relating to Parents

An important aspect of this program is the involvement and support of parents. Parents need to be informed about the program. This can be accomplished at a group meeting during which the aspects of the program are described to the parents. Or parents can be informed of the program through a special newsletter publication or a monthly calendar sent home with each child listing the sound sequence throughout the year (month).

Many families like to plan ahead. If they know when a particular sound is coming, they will have many more interesting items to offer. Often they will time outings with their children and even select birthday gifts with upcoming sounds in mind. This will also allow resource parents the chance to time their visits in advance.

The Sound of the Week and Whole Language

The programs are ultimately compatible, the embodiment of each other in theory. The exception is that *Sound of the Week* does not put as much emphasis on handwriting, mostly because it is geared to pre-writers, but, in addition, because in programs where handwriting is encouraged, required or appropriate, a program is readily available with which *Sounds of the Week* can mesh because of its

GA184

non-sequential feature. It combines the five basic elements of whole language; namely, it involves all children in:

1. using all modes of communication—reading, writing, listening, speaking, observing, illustrating, experiencing and doing.

2. the three reading cue systems: semantic (meaning), syntactic (grammatical structure), and graphaphonic (visual cues, shapes and sounds).

3. learning what takes place in whole contexts, rather than in parts.

4. actual, practical, reading and writing experiences.

5. stories with substance, meaning and sequence to draw children to read again and again from the first moment of school, for life.

Both approaches free the teacher to help children develop language skills in vital and dynamic ways, rather than by rigid sets of rules.

GA184

 # The Sound of the Week

Each sound will be dealt with as a separate unit. Not all subject matter areas are integrated into all weeks; however, the various learning areas are treated separately and always in the same sequence for ease in planning. Before planning interest areas, one must first refer to the constants described in *Constants in the Classroom Environment* (pages 3-9).

Interest Area Sequence for Each Sound Unit

> Timing and Introduction
> Special Environmental Considerations
> Whole Language, Reading and Math Readiness
> Language Arts Resources
> Activities
> Music
> Science, Health and Social Studies
> Snacks
> Special Fun
> Evaluation and Testing
> Extra Activities

The Appendix will list resource materials for music books and albums that pertain to different listings in the music sections.

 GA184

six
6
seven
7

STOP

11

GA184

The Sound of the Week is "S"

Timing

Unless you decide to proceed through *The Sounds of the Week* in alphabetical order, the letter **S** is a good **sound** with which to begin this program. **S** is easy for most children to hear, so they feel immediate **success**. If you begin *The Sound of the Week* in January as **suggested**, many key words relating to winter activities begin with the letter **S**. Of course, you could **start** in **September** or use **South** (a study of climates) as the focus or **starting** point for the letter **S**.

Special Environmental Considerations

Display **S** pictures around the classroom and label them with the appropriate **S** words. Encourage the children to begin to look for and bring their own contributions to the **S** environment. Respond to the children with **S** words **such** as **super, swell, stupendous** and **sometimes**.

Whole Language, Reading, and Math Readiness

Name Tags: Make name tags for the words **sister** and **son**. Print the words on the tags and pin them on the children as they arrive for class. This **should** be done in addition to making name tags for all **students** whose names (first or last) begin with the letter **S**.

Show-and-Tell: Children may bring things for **show**-and-tell that **start** with the letter **S**. Communication of this fact to parents is one way to eliminate a "bring-and-brag" type of **show**-and-tell. This activity **should** be a **sharing** activity. Children could hide what they bring in a **Secret Sack**. At **sharing** time the child gives hints as to the identity of the **S surprise** that is hidden inside the **sack**. Classmates can try to guess the object. Display the variety of **S** objects on a table that has been **set** aside for them. Encourage the children to examine the items and repeat the **S** names for each. Make labels for the **show** items so the children can **see** that the initial letter is the **same** for all.

Room Labels: Make cards for words that name things in the classroom that begin with the letter **S**. Children can circulate, matching cards to proper items.

GA184

Sixes and Sevens: **Six** and **seven** are two good **S** words for math activities. Both words and the numerals **should** be part of a bulletin board that contains **S** words and pictures.

Have the children draw or find **six** (or **seven**) things in the classroom that **start** with the letter **S**.

If You Were a Snowman: Discuss, graph and possibly illustrate individual answers to: "If you were a **snowman**, what would you choose for a nose (or a hat)?" Illustrations could be compiled into a group book to be **shared** with families or added to the classroom library.

Language Arts Resources

A few suggestions for correlating books are listed below. Check your library and see what books, films, poems and periodicals are available and appropriate. Look for **seasons, shoes, sun, spiders, seeds, shapes, spring, signs, snow.**

Books:
My "S" Sound Box, Jane Moncure, Children's Press, 1977.
Snowy Day, Ezra Jack Keats, Viking Press, 1962.

Poetry:
"Santa and the Reindeer," "Sara Sylvia Stout" and "Sick" are three poems that can be found in Shel Silverstein's excellent book of poetry, *Where the Sidewalk Ends*, published by Harper and Row, New York.

The Snowflake
I watched a little snowflake
As it floated round and round.
It drifted up and down and then
It fell upon the ground.
I thought it must be very cold
And lonely, too, I feared.
I brought it in to play with me
And then it disappeared.

. . . Unknown

13

The Snowman

A chubby little snowman
Had a carrot nose.
Along came a bunny
And what do you suppose?
That hungry little bunny
Looking for some lunch
Ate the snowman's carrot nose.
Nibble, nibble, crunch!

. . . Unknown

Valentine

I made a snowman yesterday
So jolly, fat and fine.
I put a red heart on his chest
And named him Valentine!

. . . Unknown

Fenceposts

Fenceposts wear marshmallow hats
On a snowy day.
Bushes in their nightgowns
Are kneeling down to pray.
And all the trees wear silver skirts
And want to dance away.

D. Aldis

Activities

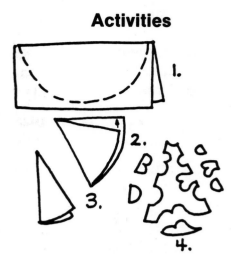

Snowflakes: Reproduce a variety of **sizes** of circles on white paper. Have the children cut out each circle, fold it in half, and then fold the half into thirds. The illustration above may help. Demonstrate how to cut out pieces to create a **snowflake** and then allow the children to make a variety to hang about the classroom.

Bleach Pictures: Each child dips a cotton **swab** into bleach and draws a **snow scene** on a piece of dark construction paper. As the bleach dries, it turns the dark paper white. Details can be added with crayons or felt pens. Be **sure** to **supply** the children with **smocks**.

Sculpture: Make clay **snowmen**. Paint hearts on the **snowmen** with nail polish. A poem to accompany this project can be found in the poetry section. It is titled "The Snowman."

Torn Snowmen: Fold a 12″ × 18″ sheet of white paper in half and make torn **snowmen**. Details can be added with crayons or by tearing and gluing bits of various colored **scrap** paper.

Sponge-Paint: Have the children draw or paint a fence on a large **sheet** of paper. Then they can **sponge**-paint the marshmallow hats, etc., that are described in the poem "Fenceposts" found in the poetry **section**.

GA184

Music

Songs:
Check music book indexes for **songs** about **snow** and other common **S** words. Traditional favorites of children include "Skip to My Lou" and "What Shall We do on a Winter's Day?" With these **songs**, **S** words like **slide, spin, stomp** and **skate** can be added to the **students'** vocabularies. The words can also be used to encourage creative movement activities.

Records:
A wide variety of recordings can be found that correlate with the **S sound**. Among the many **songs** on **Sesame Street** Records are "Be Kind to the Letter 'S'," "Sammy the Snake," "Simple Song," "Stop" and "The Sign Song." Be sure not to forget "Supercal, et.al.!"

Rhythms:
Rhythmic activities can involve imitating **snowflakes** and building **snowmen** as well as other **snow** activities **such** as **sledding, skiing** and **skating**.

Special Note: Make sure you check the Appendix on page 141 for bibliographical information concerning music books and albums.

Science, Health and Social Studies

Smell: Focus on the **sense** of **smell** through guessing games and "**Scratch and Sniff**" materials. Of course, the **sense** of **sight** also begins with the letter **S**. Another alternative would be to develop some **sound** activities.

Snow or Sand: Examine either with a magnifying glass. Do **some** experimenting. How fast will **snow** melt? How much does **sand** weigh? What are the uses for **sand** or **snow**? Which is the most important and why?

Steam: Observe and discuss as a preparation for additional activities when *The Sound of the Week* is "W."

Solids: Show ice as a **solid** form of water. Find other **solids**. Try to develop a definition of "**solid**." Classify **snow, sand** and **steam** as **solid** or not.

GA184

Snacks

If it **snows** in your area it will be great fun to make **snow** ice cream or **snow** cones.

Snow Ice Cream

Mix ⅓ cup dry powdered milk and a few drops of vanilla with a cup of clean, loose **snow**.

Snow Cones

Sprinkle pre-sweetened drink mix or Jell-O over a cup of clean, loose **snow**. Mix, eat.

Note: Chocolate instant pudding mix will help you make chocolate ice cream.

Read the book *Stone Soup* by Marcia Brown (Scribner, New York). Have the children bring the necessary vegetables. Prepare the **soup** in the classroom. Bring a **smooth, sterilized stone** for the **soup** or use bouillon cubes. Count, classify and graph the ingredients contributed.

While studying the letter **S** is a great time to make a huge, multi-ingredient **salad**. All the **students** can contribute and help cut up the vegetables.

Need **something** to accompany the **salad**? Why not **sandwiches**? Have the **students** make a list of as many kinds of **sandwiches** as they can think of. Enlist **some** parent help. Collect a variety of "fixings" and allow each **student** to create his/her own **sandwich**. Graph the children's favorite **sandwiches**.

Special Fun

For a field trip for this **sound** why not visit a **supermarket**? Look for **S** words on the labels of the various foods. Make a list of **S** things that are seen in the supermarket.

Invite a **singer, scout, sailor, seamstress** or a **salesperson** to your classroom to discuss the job he/she does. Allow the **students** time to ask any questions they might have.

Designate a day for wearing **slippers** or **stripes**.

Evaluation and Testing

To determine if the children have mastered *The Sound of the Week* try **several** of the following:

1. Can the student draw six things that **start** with the letter **S**?
2. Can the student label **seven** items in the classroom that begin with the letter **S**?

GA184

3. Given three letters, can the **student** point to the letter **S**?
4. Can the student identify the letter **S** printed in a book? Can it be found at the beginning, end, and middle of a word? Can the capital and lower case letter both be identified?
5. Can the student name **someone** in the room whose name begins with the letter **S**?
6. Can the **student** form the letter **S** in a **sand** tray?
7. Can the **student** tape the letter **S** to five items in the room that begin with the letter?

Special Note

The Problem of "sh":

Blends such as "sh," "ch," "wh," etc., can be used for later *Sounds of the Week*. They can be organized for follow-up units. During presentation of the program, **students** need to be aware that **sometimes** the letters need help from other letters to make a word. Many times the letter is "h." In this case the blend would be "**sh**." **So**, when a word begins with the letters "**sh**" and **sounds shhhhhh**, it has a very **special** place to go. Use one bulletin board area of your classroom to display the drawing below:

Have children find examples of "sh" words in print. **Shirt** and **shoe sections** of catalogs are a place to **start**, as well as picture dictionaries.

Also give each child a piece of paper with the drawing of "**sh**" duplicated on it. On this **sheet** the child **should** draw a picture of any word that begins with "**sh**." The picture **should** also be placed on the bulletin board display. The teacher can draw the pictures on the bulletin board or various children can draw the pictures as they discover new "**sh**" words.

18

19

GA184

The Sound of the Week is "J"

Timing

You may wish to schedule the letter **J** in **January** immediately after the letter **S**. The letter **J** is harder but its unfamiliarity seems to be a good challenge to this new learning style. Don't forget that **June** and **July** are also months and **J** words.

Special Environmental Considerations

"J" monograms and other suggestions are described in the *Constants in the Classroom* section that adapt well to "**J** week." This also begins to establish the routines that will provide continuity and a secure predictability about the program for the children.

Jean's Day: Designate a day when everyone is encouraged to wear jeans.

J Names: Identify classmates, friends and family members with **J** names. Make a list. Count.

Whole Language, Reading, and Math Readiness

Listening Awareness: Use the word **jingle** as a key word this week. Make up cards with words on them and allow the children to attach them to things in the room and to things they bring from home that could make a **jingling** noise.

Show-and-Tell: Reinforce the idea of bringing things to share that relate to *The Sound of the Week*. Collect and display the **J** items in a special place. Children may be ready to leave them for a day or two for extended sharing and the enjoyment of the entire class rather than taking them home the same day they are brought.

Special Note: Be sure things left for several days are labeled so they will be returned to the proper owner.

Just How Many?: For a math activity play "**just** how many?" Students guess just how many of something they think there are. This also can introduce the concepts of guessing and estimating. Ask the students to guess just how many books are in the classroom. Fill a **jar** with **jellybeans** and ask the students just how many. Spread several paper clips on the overhead projector, project the image, and ask the students just how many. Discuss the difference between guessing and estimating. What is a calculated guess?

Language Arts Resources

Books:
Books to consider using when *The Sound of the Week* is **J** include:

James and the Rain, Karla Kaskin, Harper and Row, 1957.

Jellybeans for Breakfast, Mirian Young, Parents Magazine Press, 1968.

Poetry:
"Jimmy Jet and His TV Set," from *Where the Sidewalk Ends* by Shel Silverstein, Harper and Row, is a poem your students will enjoy.

Special Note: Don't forget **Jack** and **Jill, Japan, jets** and **jokes**. Have each student tell his/her favorite **joke**. A variety of **joke** books can be found at most discount stores. Purchase a couple and read to a few children each day.

Music

Songs:
Check music resources for **J** songs, especially nursery rhymes such as "Jack Be Nimble," "Jack and Jill," "Little Jack Horner," "Jack Spratt" and "Jack-in-the-box."

Four Little Jingle Bells

Four children stand shoulder-to-shoulder to represent the side of a sleigh. As the song proceeds, each child drops a bell (in left-to-right progression) until all are gone. On "We'll pick up some new ones, and put them right on," each child picks up his/her bell and passes it to another child who replaces him/her in the line and the song continues.

Variation: Instead of dropping one bell at a time, vary the number to develop listening and number skills. For example, "Two little jingle bells fell in the snow . . ."

GA184

One Little Jingle Bell

1. Four lit-tle jin-gle bells hung in a row,
2. One lit-tle jin-gle bell fell in the snow,

1. Four lit-tle jin-gle bells help the sleigh go.
2. Three lit-tle jin-gle bells help the sleigh go.

1. Merr-i-ly, merr-i-ly, o-ver the snow
2.

1. Merr-i-ly, merr-i-ly, sleigh-ing we go!
2.

Verse 3: Repeat verse #2, dropping one more bell until all are gone.

Verse 4:
One little jingle bell fell in the snow
No little jingle bells help the sleigh go.
Slow-ly, so slow-ly the bells are all gone
We'll get some new ones and put them right on.

Records:
The songs "Jennifer of the Jungle," "J Friends," "J Jump" and "J Poem" can be found on records from Sesame Street.

Rhythm:
A variety of rhythmic activities can be designed around the J words **jump, juggle, jiggle, journey, job, jazz, jerk, jet, jive** and **jostle**.

Jumping Rope Activities: These activities can offer experience in coordination, movement, and awareness and development of stamina and rhythmic coordination. Ropes need to be six or seven feet long. Include activities such as walking along the rope on the ground forward and backward, placing the rope in a circle and operating inside or outside of it as well as jumping singly or in teams.

22

GA184

SEE HOW I'M JUMPING

See how I'm jumping, jumping, jumping. See how I'm jumping like a ball. Nobody knows I can jump so high, No-body knows I can stand so still. See how I'm jumping, jumping, jumping. When I am tired, down I flop!

Snacks

Jell-O: Plan to make **Jell-O** at school. An interesting variation is finger **Jell-O**. This is a treat which sets at room temperature rather than needing refrigeration. It can be cut into cubes or fancy shapes and should be eaten with the fingers.

To 4 cups boiling water add:

> 4 envelopes plain gelatin
> 3 large boxes of Jell-O gelatin
> Stir to dissolve
> Allow to set
> Cut into cubes

Other Snacks: When **J** is *The Sound of the Week*, other snacks could include **juice, jellybeans, jerky** and **jelly**.

GA184

Special Fun

Give each child a sheet of paper. On the paper should be several **J**'s. The child's task is to turn each **J** into something different. This exercise could be attempted several times. This will allow the child to expand his/her ability to originate ideas.

Give each child a sheet of paper. On that sheet of paper should be the letter **J**. The student's task is to use pencil, pens or crayons to add as many lines as desired to create a picture. The **J** paper has no proper top; it could be turned any way and be completed.

Evaluation and Testing

1. Identify a printed upper case and lower case **J** letter.

2. List three different **J** letter foods.

3. Identify three people with **J** names.

Extra "J" Activities

Jobs: Career awareness activities might include cutting out pictures of people working and making a collage or classifying and graphing jobs from pictures. Children could draw the **jobs** of parent(s) or "What I want to be when I grow up." Either of these is delightful when assembled into a book and shared with parents.

Journal: Keep a daily journal of class activities during **J** week. Make sure that each class member contributes to the **journal**. Let the children illustrate the pages and offer suggestions for the different writings.

Jigsaw Puzzle: The children will enjoy playing with **jigsaw** puzzles. They can work in groups or individually.

GA184

The Sound of the Week is "C"

Timing

Schedule the letter **C** early in the program since it is a letter most children already recognize. It is a natural when the weather is **cold** and many people are suffering from **coughs** and **colds**. If there is a local **circus** or **carnival**, it might be used to stimulate interest for a focus on the sound of **C**.

Special Environmental Considerations

Provide a divided display area for the two sounds of **C**. During **class** discussion, indicate that the hard **C** sound (**coughing, cat**) is the most **common** sound, but accept offerings of soft **C** words. Perhaps a sketch similar to this would be of help.

Whole Language, Reading and Math Readiness

The **ch** blend: Usually the subject of the **ch** blend **comes** up during the **C** week. When a **child** offers a **ch** word, explain the blend to everyone by writing it on a **chart** and saying, "The '**ch**' word will rest on this **chair**' or will go in this **church** along with pictures of '**ch**' words." (See the illustration below.) If **children** are ready, they may find examples of **ch** in print.

GA184

Counting: This is a good time to **check** to see how far each **child can count**. Review **counting** songs learned early in the school year or learn some now. **Children** enjoy learning to **count** backwards. Be sure to include **countdowns** to "blastoff" in activity **changes** and on the playground. **Counting** songs **could** include some of the following: "Ten Little Indians," "Fish Song," "Counting Song" and "Angel Band."

Language Arts Resources

Check resources for books, poems and films about **cars, cats, caterpillars, chickens, China, circus, clowns, colors, cooking, cookies, counting, cowboys, crabs, crickets,** and **crocodiles**.

Books:
The Very Hungry Caterpillar, Eric Carle, Collins World.
Caps for Sale, E. Slobodkina, W.R. Scott, 1947.
Carrot Seed, Ruth Krauss, Harper and Row, 1945. EASY

Poetry:

Animal crackers and cocoa to drink
This is the finest of suppers, I think
When I'm grown up and can have what I please,
I'm sure I'll always insist upon these.

A.A. Milne

Activities

Collage: Any type of **collage can** be done this week, but a **collage** of mittens for the **cold** weather would be appropriate. **Children** trace one hand in mitten form on a piece of **construction** paper and then **cut** it out. The **children** then trade their scraps with each other and draw and **cut** a second pair of mittens. (Each now has one mitten in the original color and a pair of mittens in another **color**.) Each **child** selects a background **color** from 12" × 18" paper. The children then mount their mittens in an interesting design. The mittens can be **colored** if desired.

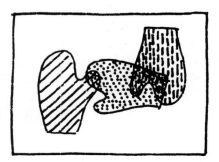

GA184

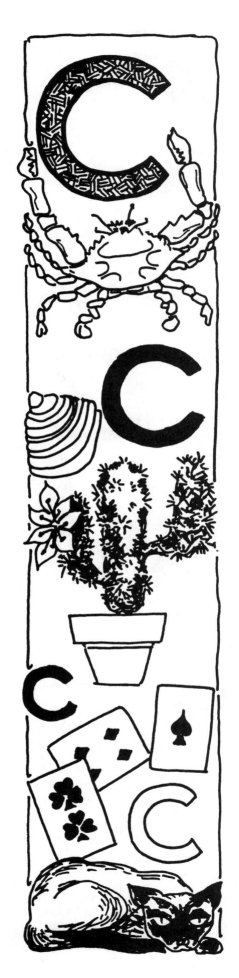

Crayon Mitten Overlay: On a sheet of 9″ × 12″ (lined) paper, the **children** trace their hands several times in mitten form. Then they fill in the patches made by the intersecting lines with different **colors**. It is fun to discuss how to vary the **coloring** techniques to add interest. It is possible for the **children** to add dots, stripes, **cross**-hatch, etc., for variation.

Caterpillar: The teacher draws a branch on a 9″× 12″ paper. Make one small **C** on the left end of the branch. The **children** then add **C**'s to the branch to make a **caterpillar**.

Rock Candy Crystals: This takes several weeks to **crystallize**. Boil together 2 **cups** sugar and 1 **cup** water until the sugar dissolves. Tie a string to a pencil and suspend it above a glass. Pour **cooled** syrup into the glass. Leave this undisturbed. **Crystals** will form along the string.

More Fun with Crystals: Observe Epsom salt **crystals** (solids) through a magnifying glass. Heat 1 **cup** water and add 4 tablespoons Epsom salts, stirring until dissolved. Add two drops of **clear** mucilage or egg white if you have it. Dab the mixture on a piece of glass, allowing some to drip off. As the water evaporates (becomes gas), the **crystals** grow again (solid). Examine it again with a magnifier. **Crystals** have become the same shape as before.

Crystal Garden: Mix in a non-metal bowl: 4 tablespoons salt, 4 tablespoons water, 4 tablespoons laundry bluing, 1 tablespoon ammonia. Pour over pieces of **charcoal** or **coal** in a shallow, non-metal dish (fish bowls work well). Place where it will not be disturbed. **Crystals** will begin to grow as liquid evaporates.

GA184

Health Activity for Coughs and Sneezes: Have the **children cut** a **circle** from a 6″ square of flesh-**colored** paper and draw a face on the **circle**. Provide yarn for hair and a tissue, which the **children** paste to the nose.

Snacks

There are several different kinds of no-bake **cookies** that **can** be made in **class**.

No-bake Cookies:
    Play-Doh **Cookies** (makes about 20)
Combine by hand: (note **count** down)
    2 **cups** honey
    3 **cups** peanut butter
    4 **cups** dry powdered milk
May form into shapes or just eat!

Cracker Cookies
(makes about 24)
Crush ⅓ lb. graham **crackers**
Mix in 1 lb. powdered sugar
Work in by hand:
  ½ lb. margarine
  1 cup peanut butter
Press into 9″ × 13″ pan.
Sprinkle on top one 12 oz. bag **chocolate chips**.
Place in sun or oven to soften **chips** for spreading if desired.
Chill. Cut.

Other snacks might include **cocoa, celery, carrots, crackers, or cupcakes**. Any or all of these **can** and should be prepared in the **classroom**.

GA184

Special Fun

The **children** might enjoy visiting a bakery and seeing **cookies** made. If a **candy** factory is nearby, visit it and let the **children** see **candy** being made.

Invite a **carpenter** to visit and perhaps demonstrate how to use his tools.

Evaluation and Testing

1. Prepare a work sheet that is divided into three sections. Have the children make four or more **C** things on the top half, and as an option to see who has grasped the soft **C** sound and the **ch** sound, have them make one soft **C** object and one **ch** object in the lower boxes.

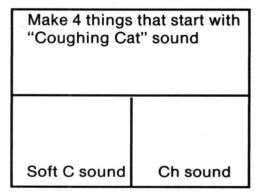

Make 4 things that start with "Coughing Cat" sound	
Soft C sound	Ch sound

2. Identify a printed **C** letter.

3. **Count** to twenty.

4. Repeat a pattern by **clapping**.

5. Name a **C** animal you might find if you went to a farm.

6. Name something you might find that starts with the letter **C** in a sweet shop.

GA184

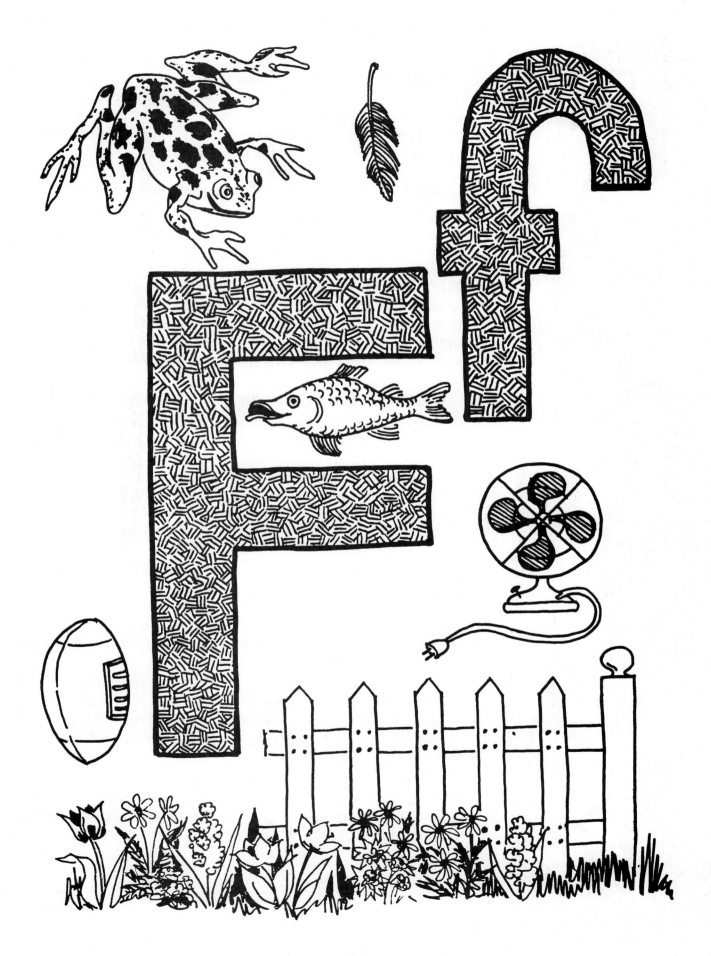

31

The Sound of the Week is "F"

Timing

This unit **fits** well during the **first** week of **February**. It also will adapt to a **festival** or **fair** week if there is one in the area. If the program is begun in the **fall**, it can adapt easily during **Fire** Prevention Week in October.

Special Environmental Considerations

Display **F** pictures, label them and provide **F** monograms. Make word cards with the word *fun* on them and have the children tape them to things they enjoy in the room. This might also stimulate a group book project with the title "**Fun**," in which each child contributes a drawing of a favorite activity. The children will enjoy sharing such a book among themselves or taking turns taking it home to share with their **families**. Respond to the children verbally using **F** words such as **fantastic, fabulous, first-rate, fine**, etc.

Whole Language, Reading, and Math Readiness

Funny Faces Book: Mount pictures of **faces from** magazines onto sheets of paper that can be inserted into a loose-leaf binder. Cut the punched pages into thirds and intermix the top thirds, the middle thirds and the bottom thirds. Then bind the book. The children open each of the three sections at any point to see a **funny face**. Then they try to make the three sections into the original pictures.

Family Room Mural: Provide a large sheet of mural paper or a pin board to which the children can add things that might be **found** in a **family** room that start with the letter **F**. Have them list **furnishings**. Ideas that may be included are **fireplace, furniture, father, family, flowers, fish, food, fork, football, February, four, five** and **face**.

Fl and Fr Words: Compile lists of **fl** and **fr** words. Check picture dictionaries and catalog indexes if necessary. Have children illustrate the words. Compile these into books the children can read!

Number Concepts of First, Four and Five: Provide opportunities for counting and grouping. **Finger** plays are a good resource here.

Language Arts Resources

Check resource materials for books, poetry and **films** dealing with **fables, farms, flags, families, fathers, firemen, fire trucks, fire prevention, flying, forests, food, frogs**, and **feelings**.

Books:

Fast Is Not a Ladybug, Miriam Schlein, W.R. Scott, 1953.
Feelings, Phoebe Dunn, Creative Education, 1971.
Five Chinese Brothers, Claire Bishop, Coward, 1938.
How Big Is a Foot?, Rolf Myller, Atheneum Pub., 1962.
My F Sound Box, Jane Moncure, Children's Press, 1977.
Story of Ferdinand, Munroe Leaf, Viking, 1936.
What Is a Fish?, Gene Darby, Benefic Press, 1958.
What Is a Flower?, Jennifer Day, Golden Press, 1975.
What Is a Frog?, Gene Darby, Benefic Press, 1957.

Activities

February Calendar: Provide each child with a calendar for the month. Emphasize the location of words such as **February** and **Friday**. Identify **first, fourth, fifth, fourteenth, fifteenth**.

Fragrant Flowers: Make paper **flowers**. Touch each with a drop of cologne. Children can wear them as boutonnieres all week.

Folded Fans: Fold 9″ × 12″ paper accordian style to make a **fan**.

Free-cut Hearts: With Valentine's Day not **far** away, this is a good week to show the children how to **free**-cut hearts without given lines. Provide an abundance of squares of several sizes and colors. Show the children how to **fold** the square and then cut it, starting near the top and cutting around as in cutting a circle; then returning in a straight line to a place near the bottom of the **fold**.

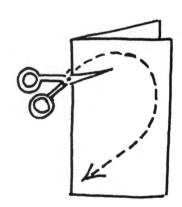

Interesting collages can be made of both the hearts and the **frames** that are left of the squares when the hearts are cut out. Mount them in random **fashion** on 9″ × 12″ construction paper.

33

GA184

Fun Flowers: (a good way to use up scraps!) **Form** a ring with a strip of paper 3″ to 6″ high. This becomes a "pot" or "basket." Children can be shown how to make the top edge more decorative with **fancy** cutting. **From** scraps of colored paper (cloth, gift wrap, etc., work well too) make **fantasy flowers** and paste on stems made from 1″ × 4″ green strips . Paste the stems around the edges of the ring as in a vase or flowerpot. Add a handle if desired to make a "basket."

Flag: A simple **flag** can be made and can be useful in honoring **famous** American birthdays in **February**. Begin with a 9″ × 12″ sheet of writing paper like the kind used in the primary grades. Cut 9″ × 12″ red paper into strips the width of the lines on the writing paper. The children paste the red strips between two lines, then leave a blank space to make white stripes. The **field** is a 4½″ × 6″ rectangle of blue, pasted in the top left corner on top of the stripes. Gummed or crayon stars may be added.

Music

Songs:
Some possible **F** letter songs that the children might enjoy singing can be **found** in the book *Music for Young Americans* by Richard Berg. They are "Family," "Fire Truck Song," "Fish Story" and "Five Little Alligators." Also, the song "Farmer in the Dell" can be found in *The Kindergarten Book* by Lilla Belle Pitts.

Records:
A number of **F** letter songs can be **found** on Sesame Street albums. They are "Fight Song," "Five People in My Family," "Four Furry Friends" and "Let a Frown Be Your Umbrella."

Science, Health and Social Studies

Families: Discuss what makes a **family**. Perhaps the children will draw pictures of their **families.**

Friends: Early in the week discuss the subject of **friends**. What does it mean to be a **friend**? At the end of the week give each child a 3″ × 5″ card on which to write his/her own name in red. The child then goes to a classmate with whom he/she would like to become a better **friend** and has the classmate sign the card in a different color.

GA184

The teacher can collect the cards and make some revealing sociometric observations about the climate in the room. **From** this might come a new seating arrangement where children could be seated with or near those whom they have chosen to befriend. Be certain to integrate all children who were not chosen at all with those who were chosen often. They might help the less sociable to become more socially acceptable to the group.

Foods: This is a good week to discuss **foods**. The teacher might discuss the difference between nutritious and junk **foods**, classify types of **food** or identify **favorite foods.**

Fish and/or Frogs: If possible, set up an aquarium and observe and care **for** different **fish** and/or **frogs**.

Fast and Slow: Provide opportunities for exploration and experimentation **for fast** and slow movements in the room, the gym or playground by using both a drum and regular music.

Flotation: Experiment with a variety of objects to see what **floats** and what does not. Help the children conclude what causes things to **float**. Provide a dishpan, wading pool or stopped sink full of water and two containers into which they can separate objects that **float** from those that don't.

For a **final** activity, have the children draw a water line through the middle of a sheet of paper. With crayons have them draw some of the things that **floated** (at water line) and some of the things that sank (at the bottom). Then do a watercolor wash to the bottom of the page to represent the water **from** the water line. Those objects which have been colored with crayons will still be visible.

Feelings: Take time during the week to discuss **feelings** and how they develop and change. Perhaps a bulletin board of pictures depicting **feelings** or a group book as described **for** the **fun** book might be appropriate. There are many books and **films** on the subject of **feelings**. Be sure to check your school resources.

GA184

Snacks

Fudge is an easy recipe that can be prepared in the classroom.

X-tra Special Fabulously Fantastic Fudge

Melt one 12-oz. package of chocolate bits. Stir in 1 can sweetened condensed milk. Add 1 teaspoon vanilla, ¼ teaspoon salt, ½ cup nuts or raisins (if desired). Spread in an 8″ square buttered pan. Chill until firm. Makes 25-30 pieces.

Other Snack Suggestions: Fortune cookies, **French fries, frankfurters, fruit, Fig** Newtons.

Flavor: This is an opportunity to discuss the meaning and significance of **flavor**. A collection of **flavors** to taste and smell is a good interest center **for** exploration this week.

Special Fun

This would be an excellent time to visit a **farm** or invite a **farmer** to visit the class. Have him discuss his profession with the children.

Take the class on a visit to a **firehouse**. Have some of the **firemen** discuss how to use the different "tools" and also have them discuss the importance of **fire** prevention.

Evaluation and Testing

1. Demonstrate your understanding of the concepts of **first, four** and **five** by reciting **finger** plays and songs.

2. **Find four** things that start with the letter **F**.

3. Identify the letter **F** in print.

4. The **Family** Room Mural (see Activities) can be used as a test. How many **F** objects can the children **find** in the mural?

Extended "F" Activity

Fingerpainting: The children will enjoy **fingerpainting**. Make sure the children have smocks or something to protect their clothing.

GA184

37

GA184

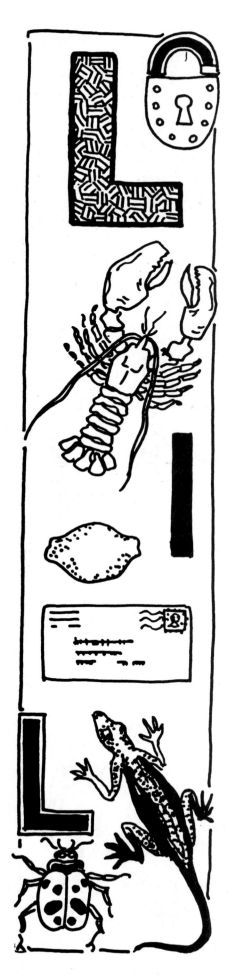

The Sound of the Week is "L"

Timing

Present the **L** sound the week of February 12, Abraham **Lincoln's** birthday. Another possibility is to present the unit in September around **Labor** Day, if you are presenting the program early in the year.

Special Environmental Considerations

Provide pictures of Abraham **Lincoln** for the children to examine. Tell them stories of **Lincoln's** childhood and read them poems about **Lincoln**. Have pictures and stories of other famous Presidents as well for comparison.

Whole Language, Reading, and Math Readiness

Less: Emphasize the concepts of more and **less** in as wide a variety of areas as possible: numbers, weight, **length**, age, money, time, etc.

Long and Short: Provide experiences in comparison of **lengths**, both of concrete objects and **lengths** of time.

Little and Big, Large and Small: Provide word cards for **little** and **large** for the children to attach to objects around the room.

Language Arts Resources

Check sources for books, films and poems about **Lincoln**, **leaves, light, ladybugs,** and the **Lion** and Mouse fable.

Books:
Ladybird Quickly, Juliet Kepes, Little, 1964.
Leaf Book, Anne Orange, Lerner, 1975.
Lentil, Robert McCloskey, Viking, 1940.
Letter to Amy, Keats, Viking, 1962.
Lion, William DuBois, Viking, 1956.

Activities

Left and Right Activities: Learn to distinguish **left** from right through finger plays and rhythmic routines such as the following example.

This is my right hand
I hold it high.
This is my left hand
I touch the sky.

Right hand, left hand
Round and round.
Left hand, right hand
Pound, pound, pound.

GA184

This is my right foot
Tap, tap, tap
This is my left foot
Pat, pat, pat.
Right foot, left foot
Run, run, run.
Left foot, right foot
Jump for fun.

Right face, left face
Turn round and round.
Left face, right face
Jump up and down.
Right hand, left hand
Clap, clap, clap.
Right foot, left foot
Tap, tap, tap.

Let's have fun.
Now begin . . .
With your left hand
Touch your chin.
With your right hand
Touch your head.
Left on your knee,
Now right instead.
With your left hand
Touch your ears.
Now clap both hands
And give three cheers!

1-10 Ladybugs: Prepare a page of 10 **ladybugs** with no spots, in grass. On red, prepare cutouts of 10 **ladybug** bodies with 1-10 dots on each back. Children cut out red **ladybug** bodies and paste each on the correctly numbered **ladybug** in the grass (see sample).

Hinged Ladybug: Duplicate on red a **ladybug** body and wings. Children cut out and attach the wings with a fastener. Challenge activity: Draw or write **L** things on the body to be exposed when the wings open (see sample).

Lilac: Prepare 1″ squares of **lilac** tissue paper and a few green heart or oval shapes for **leaves**. Each child draws a branch, applies paste along part of it, and pinches tissue squares onto the paste to make blossoms. Add a few **leaves** at the bottom of the branch (see sample).

(See Lion and Leopard in **Z Week**, pp.104-105)

Music

Songs: Sing and play the classic "Did You Ever See A Lassie?"
The **L** letter songs "Abraham Lincoln" and "Looby Lou" can be found in the book *Music for Young Americans* by Richard Berg (refer to Appendix for bibliography).

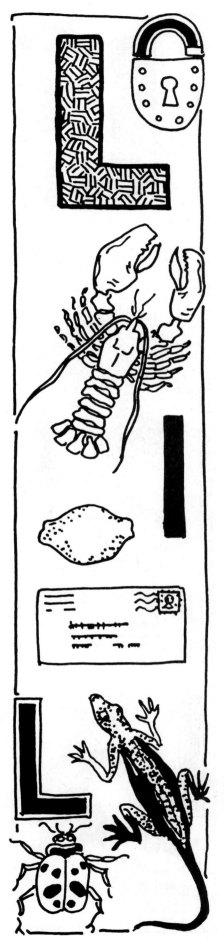

GA184

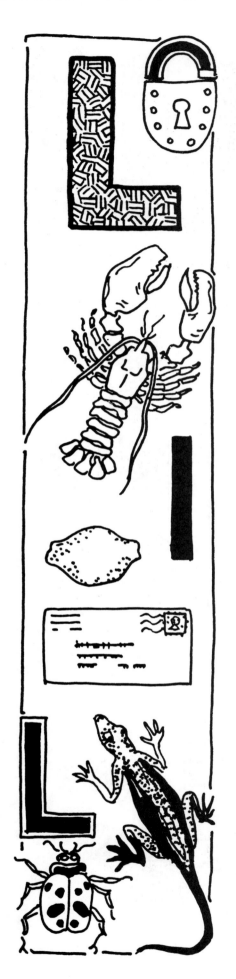

Records:
A number of albums have **L** letter songs. "La La La" and "Loud & Soft" can be found on Sesame Street Records. "The Ballad of Lucy Lum" can be found on the album *The Ballad of Lucy Lum* by Good Apple.

Science, Health and Social Studies

Locks: Have the children bring an assortment of **locks** and keys for manipulation.

Ladybugs: Ladybugs are always of interest to children. Seek out books and films in your resources.

Living and Non-Living Things: Through discussion help the children to see that all things are either **living** or non-living. Establish criteria for **living** things. To be alive, things must eat, grow and reproduce.

Light Activities and Discoveries: Make a picture display of different kinds of **light**. Discuss how **light** helps us and hurts us (too much sun, etc.).

Hold various materials next to a window to see if **light** can pass through them. Try different kinds of paper such as waxed paper, tissue paper, cellophane and crepe paper.

Discuss ways **light** differs in brightness and think of examples such as theater **lights**, candlelight, flashlight, flash bulb, stadium **lights**, car **lights**, dental chair **light**, floodlights, etc.

Light a candle in a safe place in the room before any children arrive. **Light** the room as usual. See how **long** it takes for anyone to notice the candle. Extinguish the **light** and note the contrast.

Snacks

Lettuce, licorice, lemons, limes and **lollipops** would all be easy snacks to prepare.

Evaluation and Testing

1. Draw four things that start with the **letter L**.
2. Identify the upper and **lower** case **letter L** in print.
3. Differentiate between your right hand and **left** hand and your right foot and **left** foot.

GA184

41

The Sound of the Week is "V"

Timing
Valentine's Day week is a natural for presentation of the letter **V**.

Special Environmental Considerations
If possible, obtain examples of old-fashioned **valentines** from a library or collectory. Have the word *valentine* available for copying. How many words can the children make using the letters from the word *valentine*?

Whole Language, Reading, and Math Readiness

Valentine Book: Teach the children a **valentine** song. One song that might be used is "Making **Valentines**" by John Beattle (refer to the Appendix for bibliography). On one day give each child two sheets of 12" × 18" newspaper folded into a book. On the cover paste a copy of the words to the **valentine** song (or use a **verse** of a **valentine** poem). Skip the back of the cover page. Beginning on the next page, have them put two, then three, then four hearts. On the last page have them make "plenty more" and paste them on. Recognize those children who make the most. Staple the book together.

Increasing and Decreasing Order: Prepare a master containing five or six hearts of different sizes. Make two pages for each child. On Monday give the children one sheet to cut out and arrange on a 6" × 18" strip in increasing order. The next day give them the other sheet to arrange in decreasing order. Discuss and demonstrate the concept with the children. Nested bowls and blocks could be used instead of **valentines**.

Language Arts Resources
Check the library for books, films and poems about **violets, veterinarian, vegetables, violin, valentines** and **volcanos**. Read the classic *Velveteen Rabbit* (Williams, 1926).

Poetry:
> I made a snowman yesterday
> So jolly, fat and fine.
> I put a red heart on his chest
> And named him Valentine.

> Unknown

GA184

Valentine Mail

When the mailman came,
I ran to see,
If he had brought
Some mail for me.

Surprise! The letters
All were mine,
And every one,
A Valentine!

Leland V. Jacobs

I made some valentines from bread
Dad hung them on a tree
The hearts all said
To the hungry birds
"This treat's to you
From me."

Leland B. Jacobs
(*Early Years* magazine 2/81)

Valentines

I have valentines
Pink and white and
lacy.
I have valentines
Bright and funny
face-y.
I have valentines
Golden brown and
sweet.
I won't have them
very long
Because they are to
eat.

Pearl H. Watts

If I Could Be

If I could be a valentine
All red and gold and white,
If I could be a valentine
I'd wish with all my might
That I could choose the person
That I'd be given to.
I know exactly who I'd choose:
Y-O-U

Leland B. Jacobs

Activities

Snowman Valentine: Use the clay snowman made during **S** week or make one of paper to accompany the poem under the poetry section.

Valentines: Give the children time and materials to create **valentines** for friends and classmates.

Vases of Violets: The children draw a **vase** of **violets**, then put a **violet** wash of paint over all. The **vase** can be decorated with a pattern of handwritten **V**'s.

43

Valentine Mail Bag: Provide each child with a receptacle for **valentines** by folding a sheet of 12″ × 18″ paper like an envelope. Punch the three sides. Tie yarn to the first hole on one side and knot the free end of the yarn. The yarn can be pushed through the punched holes so the children can easily sew the bag. Decorate the bag with hearts.

Bleach on Red Paper: Using bleach on cotton swabs, have the children draw on red paper. As the paper dries, the bleaching reveals an attractive design. Encourage the children to make a **valentine** motif. Provide them with smocks.

Heart Butterfly Valentine: Duplicate hearts on 9″ × 12″ paper as shown. Give each child one red sheet and provide one pink sheet or one white sheet for every two children. The children cut out the two red hearts and one white or one pink heart. The white or pink heart is then cut in half. Pieces are arranged to form a butterfly. The body is made from a 6″ × 1″ strip. The wings are decorated with free-cut hearts (see **F** week Activities).

Music

Check different resources for **Valentine** songs and rhythms. Play some recorded love songs. Listen to an album with **violin** or **viola** music.

Snacks

Vegetables, Velveeta and **vanilla** pudding are a **few** good snacks for the letter **V**.

Valentine Lunch in School: One calm way to have a room party is to make it a luncheon. The children can prepare red Jell-O, make and decorate cookies, bring a sandwich from home and buy milk. Placemats and napkins can be made too. Consider an "I Love You" lunch for the principal, nurse, librarian, custodian, etc.

Special Fun

Visit an animal hospital or invite a **veterinarian** to **visit** the class. The children might enjoy inviting him to stay for lunch (see snacks).

Evaluation and Testing

1. Name four foods that begin with the letter **V**.
2. Identify a **V** object from an assortment of objects.

44

two
2
ten
10
three
3

The Sound of the Week is "T"

Timing

National Dental Health Week, usually the first week in February, is a good week to **teach** the sound of **T**. The instructor can focus the study on **teeth**.

Special Environmental Considerations

Obtain a model of **teeth** and a **toothbrush** from the school nurse or a local dentist. Also, have the children bring **their toy telephones.** Respond to children with **T** words such as **tremendous** and **terrific**.

Whole Language, Reading and Math Readiness

The "T" Book: Duplicate pages for the children to color, assemble and read. **The** following are examples of pages **that** can be included in **the** book.

The truck tows the trailer to the tent.

The two Teddys use the telephone.

The toy train travels to town.

Two tigers take ten turtles to tea.

GA184

Trains: Paper **trains** can be adapted to many math and reading activities such as counting, ordering, etc.

Oral Language Development: Have the children do **the** following: name some **toys**; repeat a **telephone** number; practice **talking** and word pronunciation on a **toy telephone**; **tell** jokes; name a favorite **television** program; name a kind of **truck**.

Toy Shelf Exercise: Place **toys** on shelves and have the children identify **their** positions by using such words as **top**, middle, behind, beside, etc.

Two and Ten: Introduce **the** concepts of **two**, pairs, and **twins**, and **the** concept of **ten** by using a calendar and groups of children.

Triangles: Have **the** children attach **triangles** to **triangular** shaped objects in **the** room. Provide the children with different **triangular** shapes and have **them** make different designs.

Games: Teach the children to play games such as **Tic Tac Toe** and **Tag**.

Language Arts Resources

Check resources for stories, poems and films about **trees**, **trains, Tooth** Fairy, **tools, twins, teachers, teeth, tigers, toys** and **trucks**.

Poetry:

Tooth
I lost a tooth the other day
And now my smile looks queer.
But I am growing one brand new
And it will soon be here.
My daddy had to have one pulled
And he can't grow it new
I'd like to give him my old one
But he says that it just won't do.

10 Tall Trees (handplay)
The wind blew through my ten tall trees
And made them bow and bend
It raced about and picked them up
And made them straight again.
Five tall trees reached to the sky
Five bent in an arch
And round and round they blew around
In the windy month of March.

47

GA184

The following poem can be used with **the turtle** activity.

A House for One
The turtle children
Sister and brother
Do not live in one house
With their father and mother.
Each baby turtle
Is happy alone
In a snug little house
All his very own.

Laura Arlon

Activities

Tissue Overlay: Apply liquid starch **to** construction paper. Layer on pieces of colored **tissue** paper. Encourage overlapping of **the** colors and discussion concerning **the** resulting secondary colorations. Allow **to** dry. **This** same **technique** can be done on waxed paper and, after drying, can be pressed with a warm iron **to** form a stained-glass effect.

Truck Tracks: Dip **toy trucks** in shallow **trays** of paint and make designs by running **the trucks** on **the** paper. Observe different **tread tracks**.

Take-Apart Table: Collect out-of-order appliances, kitchen gadgets, clocks, etc., for **the** children **to** dismantle. Use of small **tools** such as pliers, screw drivers and wrenches is good for small muscle development. (Cut **the** plugs off **the** appliances before **the** children start, so **they** don't **try to** plug **them** in!)

Three Bear Book: **This** activity is a review of geometric shapes and story sequence. **The** children read **through the** book's facing pages, **then** return **to the** beginning and finish **the** story by reading **the** backs of **the** pages as shown. **The** book is made from pre-cut geometric shapes of paper. (See **the** illustrations on **the** following pages.)

Resource: "Song Story," Lilla Belle Pitts, *The Kindergarten Book*, Ginn & Co., New York, 1959.

Turtles: Lay **two** strips of construction paper for legs and a piece of **thread** for a pull into half a walnut shell. Put in a small bit of clay. Press a marble into **the** clay and pull.

48

GA184

The Three Bears

Review of Geometric
Shapes & Story Sequence
1.

Back of cover

2.

Back of 2.

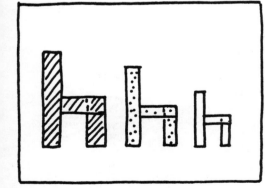

3.

Back of 3.

49

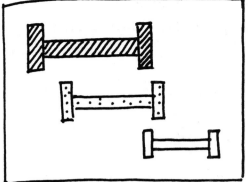

4.

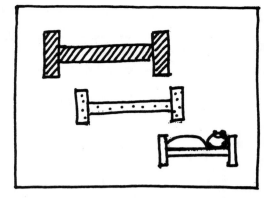

Back of 4.

5.

6" X 1"

5" X 3/4"

4" X 1/2"

Pink House, Baby Bear's bowl, chair, bed

Music

Songs:

"Little Johnny Had a Toothbrush" (sung **to the tune** of "My Darling Clementine")

Little Johnny

Little Johnny had a toothbrush
Left it hanging on the wall.
And it hung there and it hung there
For he used it not at all.

Til one day at the table
He began to scream and cry
"Mother dear, I have a toothache!
Mother dear, I think I'll die!"

So she took him to the dentist
But the dentist shook his head
"It's too late for little Johnny
Should have brushed his teeth instead."

The song "Me and My Teddy Bear" can be found on Peter Pan Records.

GA184

Science, Health and Social Studies

Teeth: Discuss dental hygiene, including proper brushing and flossing of **teeth**. Also discuss proper nutritional habits and how **they** relate to dental care.

Adopt a Tree: Late winter science activities can focus on the beginning **transition** of **trees** in spring.

Fingerprint a Tree: Take rubbings of bark. What does bark do for **the** tree? Why is bark rough and scaly? Is bark dead or living material?

Date a Tree Stump: Count the rings on a rubbing. How old is **the tree**? Why are some rings wider **than** others? How can we account for scars in **the** wood?

Adopt a Bud: Tie yarn on a **terminal (tip)**bud. Observe **the** swelling. Compare it with other buds or dead **twigs**. Note how many branches grow in a year. Compare a **tree's** growth with **the** growth of **the** children in a five year period. Observe **the** bud weekly during **the** spring.

Tulips: Provide each child with a 6″ square. Fold it into fourths. Open it. Place a quarter coin in **the** center and **trace** around it. Cut on **the** four folds from **the** edge **to the** line made by **tracing the** quarter. Overlap **the** corners and paste **them to** form a **tulip** head. Fasten **this to** a sturdy paper or pipe cleaner stem (see sample).

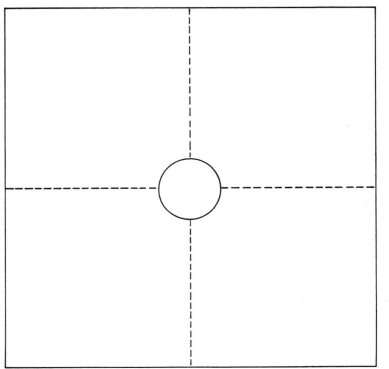

Snacks

Some possible **T** letter snacks are **Trix, taffy, tapioca** (pudding), **toast, tea, tangerines, tuna,** and **Teddy** Graham cereal.

51

Special Fun

Teddy Bear Day: On **Tuesday** of **T** week allow **the** children **to** bring **their teddy** bears (or other stuffed **toys**) **to** school **to** honor **their** faithfulness **through the** years. Sing **teddy** bear songs, hold a parade or have **the** children dance with **them**. Serve **tea** and **triangular toast** at **ten** o'clock or at **two** in **the** afternoon.

Truck Day: Encourage **the** children **to** bring a **truck to** school. Arrange **the trucks** in a **truck** show. Discuss each one and award a ribbon **to** fit an outstanding characteristic of each **truck**.

Bring in a dentist or **the** school nurse **to** discuss proper care of **teeth**.

Have a **typist** visit **the** class. Borrow a **typewriter** for **the** children **to** use. Perhaps **the** school has an old discarded one **that** can be donated **to the** class.

Evaluation and Testing

1. Draw or find **two, three** or **ten things that** start with **the** letter **T**.
2. Identify the letter **T** in print.
3. Draw or point **to three triangular**-shaped objects.
4. Complete **the** following work sheet.

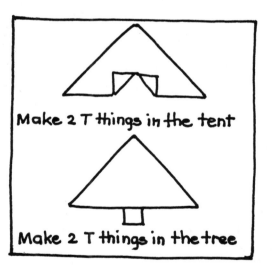

Make 2 T things in the tent

Make 2 T things in the tree

Special Note: If **the** problem of **the Th** sounding words comes up, it can be **treated** in a manner similar **to the treatment** of **sh** or **ch** words. Simply put all **th** words into a **thimble**, **theater** or **thermos** bottle because **they** will be dealt with later.

GA184

53

GA184

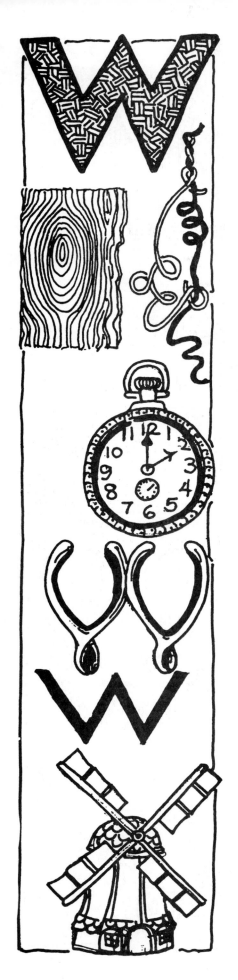

The Sound of the Week is "W"

Timing

Present the sound of **W** as close as possible to George **Washington's** birthday, **while** the **weather** is still **wintry**.

Special Environmental Considerations

Provide several **Washington word** cards to be attached to pictures of the famous American. **When** talking **with** the children, respond to them **with** positive **W** sounding **words** such as **wow, wonderful** and **winner**.

Whole Language, Reading, and Math Readiness

How Does It Go? Mural: Discuss **with** the children the many **ways** that things that begin **with** the letter **W** move, such as **walk, wiggle, wings, wind, waddle, wheels, wheelbarrow, worm, whale** and **windmill**. Have everyone prepare the background mural. Let the children paint, draw and cut out different pictures that start **with** the letter **W** to put on the mural. Label the pictures with the appropriate corresponding **word**.

Language Arts Resources

Check resources for books, films, and poems about **Washington, wind, wheels, winter** and **whales**.

Poetry:

The Wind

The wind has blown the clouds away
And brushed the sky with blue.
It stirred up mischief yesterday
And still is at it, too.

It has done its best to shake
The leaves from our old tree.
And now it's trying hard to make
A windmill out of me.   (windmill arms)

Wind Handplay

The wind blew through my ten tall trees (fingers up)
And made them bow and bend. (sway hands back and forth)
It raced about and picked them up
And made them straight again. (fingers up straight)
Five tall trees reached for the sky (one hand up)

GA184

Five bent in an arch (bend at wrist)
And round and round they blew around (alternate up and down)
In the windy month of March.

Unknown

Activities

George Washington: Center some activities around George **Washington**. Have the children draw a silhouette of him. Have the children draw or make three-cornered George **Washington** hats.

Wood Rubbings: Place paper over samples of **wood** and, using peeled crayons, rub the **wood** to get the print of the grain, bark, knots, etc.

Wire Sculpture: Request scraps of **wire** from the parents of the children. Or, ask for **wire** scraps from the telephone company. The children can randomly twist them into free sculpture which may be hung for a mobile or mounted on a board.

Music

Songs: Check music book indexes for songs about **water, wind, winter** and **weather**.

"George Washington," *Music for Young Americans* by Richard Berg, is one possible **W** letter song.

Records: Sesame Street Records has **W** letter songs such as "Washington and Lincoln" and "National Association of W-Lovers."

Rhythms: Young People's Records has **W** songs **with** good rhythm and beat. A couple are "Winter Fun" and "My Playmate the Wind."

Science, Health and Social Studies

Water: Observe **water** as a solid, liquid and gas. Melt ice in a container and place it in the sun to evaporate.

Lay a piece of ice on paper. Trace its shape. Let it melt.

Trace and compare the **wet** spot **with** the original shape.

Let an ice cube melt in a cup. Then, refreeze the **water** in the cup. Observe and discuss the differences and similarities.

Wind: Have the children make their own kites or **wind** socks **with which** to run (see kites, pp. 58-59).

GA184

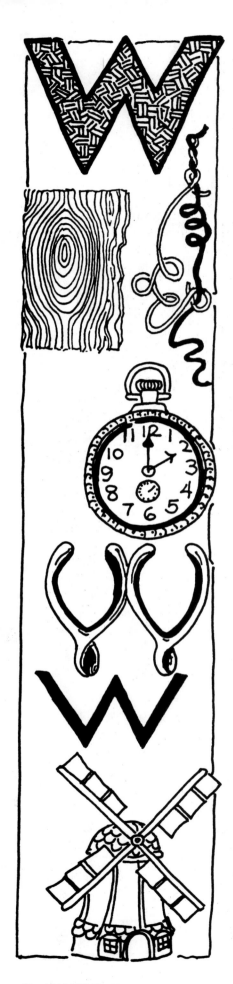

Wheels: Collect different types of **wheels**. Provide inclined planes and ramps for experimenting. Make **Wednesday** "**Wheel** Day." Let the children bring different toys **with wheels** for a show.

Wood: Observe several kinds of **wood** such as sticks, lumber, driftwood, etc. Note the different sizes, shapes, kinds and uses of each.

Make nail pictures by pounding nails into scrap **wood** in a design. Then twist the nails **with** yarn or rubber bands.

Wonder Walk: Take the children on a "**Wonder Walk**." Have each child take an egg carton along and fill the compartments to match the poem below. Reproduce the poem and paste it into the egg carton lid.

Wonder Walk

Something green
Something brown
Something for a fairy crown.
Something hard
Something yellow.
Something shiny, my young fellow.
Something long
Something wide
Something with something else inside.
Something smooth
A bit of down.
Something that should have stayed in town.
(litter)

Snacks

Let the children be **waiters** and **waitresses** during snack time.

Some possible **W** snacks that they might serve are **walnuts, waffles, whipped cream, wheat, wieners** and **watermelon**.

Evaluation and Testing

1. Draw four things that start **with** the letter **W**.
2. Draw four things with wheels that start **with** the letter **W**.
3. Point to a **W** object.
4. Identify one of the **W** sounding actions on the *How does It Go? Mural* (Page 54).

GA184

57

GA184

The Sound of the Week is "K"

Timing

Schedule the sound of **K** early in March or during another windy season for an emphasis on activities with kites.

Special Environmental Considerations

Plan to have a **kite** display. Collect and show as many **kites** as possible from foreign countries or have the children make **kites** as a family project at home. Have them bring their **kites** to school for judging near the end of the week. Awards can be made for biggest, smallest, prettiest, best flier, etc.

Language Arts Resources

Check resources for stories about **kittens, kings, kites** and **kangaroos**.

Poetry:
I sailed my kite so high
I thought that it would touch the sky.
It danced about and dived so low
And then it waved to let me know
It was such fun up in the blue
It wished that I could be there too!

Unknown

A Funny Kite Poem
I am a kite, high in the sky,
Floating along on the wind.
And the funniest thing,
I'm holding a string,
With a child on the other end!

Activities

Fish Kite: This is a simplified version of Japanese paper folding. The finished product is a mobile for hanging inside, rather than a kite to fly.

Fold a 12″ × 18″ piece of construction paper as shown in the illustration and staple.
Fold two 3″ squares in half and cut into rings.
Paste one ring for the mouth of the fish.
Cut the other ring in half for the gills.
For scales, use the scraps from cutting the circles.

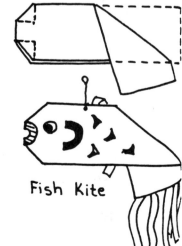

Fish Kite

GA184

The centers of the rings can be used for the eyes.
Add tissue strips for the tail and fins.
Hang the fish **kite** with thread.

Scoop Kite: This simple **kite** flies behind a running child, from the handlebars of a bike or from an antenna.

Fold a 9″ square of construction paper in half diagonally. Open it and bring the two non-folded corners together forming a cone.
Paste or staple the seam.
Attach a string.
A "tail" can be made from ribbon, yarn or other streamers.

Sack Kite: Making this **kite** can be integrated with a clean-up project of the school grounds.

Fold a 1″ cuff around the top of a large sack.
Attach scrap paper and streamers as decorations.
Attach a 36″ piece of string to the cuff.
To fly the **kite**, the children must run and fill it with air. As the children return to class, have them fill their sacks with litter from the school yard.

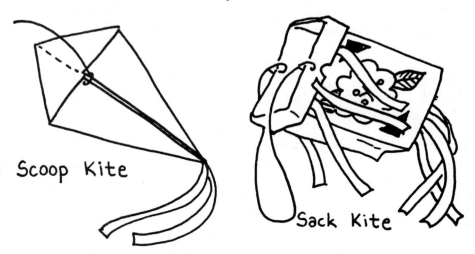

Scoop Kite

Sack Kite

Kangaroo: Duplicate a **kangaroo** shape with a separate pocket to attach. Have children make the **kangaroo** and then draw or find pictures of **K** things to put in the pocket. Some might write **k** words to include.

Music

Records:

Sesame Street Records has **K** letter songs such as "K Poem." Another song that the children would enjoy singing is "Old King Cole."

GA184

The children might also enjoy learning the following song:

THE KIND KANGAROO

Said the kind kangaroo, "Oh, what shall I do?
If I had a cradle I'd rock it.
But I think after all, since my baby's so small,
I'll carry it round in my pocket."

Snacks

Kix, Kool-aid, kisses, kabobs, kraut and **kumquats** are possible snack ideas for this unit.

Krumkake (Norwegian Cookie)
Beat 3 eggs
Add ½ cup sugar, ½ cup melted butter, 1 teaspoon vanilla
Blend in ½ cup flour

Bake on preheated **krumkake** iron 1-2 minutes until delicately brown. Roll immediately into a cone shape. Eat plain or fill with whipped cream.

Special Fun

Kitten Day: Since spring is the time of the year for **kittens**, this is a good time to invite a family of **kittens** to come to visit your class. A display of stuffed or ceramic toy kittens could be made by the children. Ribbons could be awarded for various categories of kittens.

Evaluation and Testing

1. Prepare a duplicated drawing of a large **kite** divided into four sections. Have the children draw or cut out four **K** things, one for each section.

2. Have each child identify the upper and lower case **K** in print.

GA184

purple

61

The Sound of the Week is "P"

Timing

The letter **P** can be presented in the spring with emphasis on **puddles, pansies** and **popping.** If **presented** in the fall, emphasis can be **placed** on **pumpkins, puddles, Pilgrims** and **popcorn.** Or, **presentation** of the unit during the winter can emphasize **penguins.**

Special Environmental Considerations

Display **pictures** and examples of **pairs** around the room. Encourage the children to bring things to add to the display. **Pots** of **pussy** willows will be useful in many activities during the week. The sound of **P** can be called the **popping** sound. Responses to the children should include **P** words such as **perfect** and **pretty.** Use **pink** and **purple** wherever **practical.**

Whole Language, Reading, and Math Readiness

Perceptual Puzzles: The children are given two copies of a shape. Have them cut one out and then cut it into several **pieces** (3-6). The **pieces** are then reassembled on the uncut **pattern.** This can be done with all the familiar geometric shapes such as circles, squares, rectangles, triangles, ellipses and rhombuses.

Predicting outcomes: Using stories or **pictures,** discuss what will happen next or how it will end.

Pairs: Define the word **pair.** Collect **pairs** of objects such as salt and **pepper** shakers, a **pair** of gloves, or a **pair** of glasses, shoes or socks. Have the children observe and handle as many **pairs** as **possible,** and have them discuss their discoveries.

Language Arts Resources

Check books, poems and films for **P** letter subjects such as **Pilgrims, plums, puppies, plants, penguins, Paul** Bunyan, **Pecos** Bill, **Paddington** Bear, **Peter Pan,** Winnie the **Pooh, Pinocchio, poison prevention** and **playground** safety.

GA184

Books:
Peter's Long Walk, Barbara Cooney, Doubleday, 1953.
Pilgrim's Party, Lowitz, Grossett & Dunlop, 1932.
Pussywillow, Leonard Weisgard, Golden Press, 1951.
Story About Ping, Marjorie Flack, Viking, 1933.

Poetry:

Poem for Pussy Willow Finger Painting
Tiny little pussy willow
Softer than a baby's pillow
Sometimes when I stroke your furr
I can almost hear you purr.

Unknown

Popcorn Action Poem
Pop is how the weasel goes,
Pop means "in you scoot,"
Pop is how you smash a bag,
Or firecrackers shoot.

Pop is how the toast gets up,
Pop is what you drink.
Pop is someone's father too,
But best of all, I think
Is popcorn
Poppity, pop, pop, pop,
Filling the pan
Up to the top.
(Children pop up on the word *pop*.) Unknown

Shel Silverstein's book, *Where the Sidewalk Ends,* has **P** letter **poems**. A couple are "Pancake" and "Peanut Butter Sandwich."

Pussywillow Sensory Experience
Have children close their eyes while you walk around the room and stroke their cheeks with the pussywillow and chant the following rhyme:

Close your eyes.	Smooth as satin,
Don't you peek!	Soft and sleek.
I'll rub spring	Close your eyes.
Across your cheek.	Don't you peek!

Activities

Paint Experiments: Experiment with mixing colors when **painting**. Show the children how to mix red and white to make **pink**, red and blue to make **purple**, and red and yellow to make orange. Check resources for further information about mixing colors. Have only **pink** or **purple paint** available for a day or so.

GA184

Puppets: The children will enjoy making stick, finger, **potato**, sack and other **puppets**.

Pilgrim Portraits: Have the children cut and **paste** a **Pilgrim** boy or girl for a stand-up decoration.

Pussy Willow Finger Painting: Paint over a sheet of **paper** with brown fingerpaints. Finish by having the children drag their fingernails up from the bottom of the sheet to form bush-like lines. On the second day, have the children dip their finger tips into gray **paint** and **print** on the bushes to make **pussy** willows (see the illustration). A pussy willow poem can be attached to the picture. This can be found in the **Poetry** section.

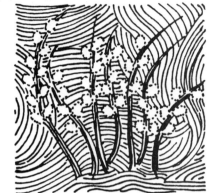

Popcorn Blossoms: Glue **popcorn** to bare twigs. The blossoms can be colored by shaking **powdered** tempera over them. (Be certain not to butter the **popcorn** or it may not stick with the glue.)

Policeman: Paste together a **policeman precut** from geometric shapes. The head is a circle cut from a 6″ square. The hat, arms and legs are 3″ × 6″ rectangles. The body is a 9″ square. The hat brim is a 1″ × 6″ strip with corners cut off. Add a ¼″ gold strip for a braid if desired. Add a gummed star for a badge and have the children trace their own hands on a folded **piece** of 9″ × 6″ white **paper**. Then have the children cut these out to make white gloved hands for their **policemen** (see illustration).

Music

Songs:
There are several **P** letter songs. Check different song book indexes for their listings. *The American Singer, Book I* by John Beattle, American Book Co., New York, has the songs "Pop Goes the Weasel" and "Pussy Willow." Also, the book *My Picture Book of Songs* by Alene Dalton, M.A. Donahue, New York, has the song "Pitter Pat."

GA184

Records:
Sesame Street Records has the songs "My Favorite Letter P," "Pat, Pat Patty Pat," "Patty Cake Gorilla" and "Peter and the Wolf."

Special Note: Check sources for songs about **puppies, ponies, parrots** and **partridges**.

Science, Health and Social Studies

Plants: Have the children bring in odds and ends of seeds and cuttings that will root and begin **plant** experiments.

Plant radish seeds or lettuce seeds in a deep container with **plans** to harvest them during the **R** week or at the end of school.

Poison Control Centers: Through discussion, films, and stories, acquaint the children with safety standards related to **poisoning**. Local hospitals, **Poison** Control Centers and the school nurse often have materials related to this subject. **Provide** the children with information for contacting a **Poison** Control Center in case of emergency.

Puddles: If **possible**, wait for a rainy day and go outside and actually observe **puddles**. Develop discussion using questions such as:

> Where do **puddles** come from?
> Are they really made of water?
> Is there anything else in them?
> Why don't we always have **puddles**?
> Are they good or bad for the **playground**?
> What is the temperature of a **puddle**?
> Do all **puddles** last the same amount of time?
> Is the mudddy-looking stuff dirt?
> Do weather and wind affect how fast they go away?
> What can you add to make it go away faster?
> Why don't grownups like **puddles**?
> Why do kids like them?

Puddle Activities: Draw circles from 12" to 18" in diameter on the floor or **playground**. Allow one foot of space between them. Have the children follow commands such as: in the **puddle**, over the **puddle**, straddle the **puddle**, two in a **puddle**, sit in the **puddle**, tip toe around the **puddle**, etc. Have the children **pretend** to be people, animals, ducks, balls, **pebbles**, etc., and show how each reacts in response to a **puddle**.

65

Three in a Puddle: Some children are grouped in threes in a specific number of circles (puddles). At the sound of a whistle, all the children in circles must change to different **puddles**. The children standing on the outside try to get in one of the **puddles** (circles).

Snacks

Make **peanut** butter, **popcorn, pumpkin pies** and roast **pumpkin** seeds.

Other foods to serve might include **peanuts, pineapples, peppers, pickles, pears** and **potato** chips.

Special Fun

Resource People: Invite a **policeman** and **pom pon** girls to visit the class. Have them discuss their "responsibilities" with the children.

Patched Pants Day: Invite the children to wear **patched** clothing on Friday. Award prizes for the most **patches**, the **prettiest patches**, etc. Make sure that each child that **participates** is awarded a **prize**.

Piano Concert: Many children can **play** a tune on the **piano**. Discuss musical terms, concerts, concert manners, applause, respect and quiet with the children. Let the children have a concert **performance** with solos and duets.

Picnic: Plan a **picnic** adventure with the children. A menu might include **peanut** butter sandwiches on **pumpernickel** bread, **pickles, peppers, pears, peaches, potato** chips and **pop. Parents** and **preschoolers** might be invited.

Pink and Purple Days: Children are encouraged to wear these colors on those days. Use **paint and paper** and have snacks of those colors.

Evaluation and Testing

1. Draw four **pictures** that start with the **popping** sound.
2. Identify the upper and lower case **P** in **print**.
3. Name different objects that come in **pairs**.

GA184

GIRLS

GO

GREEN

green

GA184

The Sound of the Week is "G"

Timing

Schedule the sound of **G** in March to coincide with St. Patrick's Day and the **greening** of spring. Another possibility is February 2, **Ground** Hog Day.

Special Environmental Considerations

Use **green** in the classroom environment wherever possible, when using pencils, chalk or even scratch paper. Respond to the children with **G** words such as **great, good, gorgeous, gigantic** and **glorious**.

Whole Language, Reading, and Math Readiness

Name Tags: Make **guys** and **girls green** name tags. And also make name tags for any proper names that start with the letter **G**.

Sight Words: Children should be introduced to the sight words **go** and stop. They should also be able to distinguish between the two.

Word Cards: Attach green cards with the word green on them to **green** objects in the classroom or environment.

Good News: As an oral activity, discuss experiences of receiving **good** and bad news.

Math Readiness: Schedule **grouping** activities. **Group** different articles by color or by their shade of **green, gold** or **gray**.

Goldfish Counting Game: Provide each child with about 20 **goldfish** shaped crackers.
The teacher tells a story about a hungry shark that swims about in the big ocean. From time to time the shark opens its jaws and **gobbles** up a stated number of the little **goldfish** from the sea. After several "meals," when the number of **goldfish** left is recognizable by the students, the teacher can say how many the shark will eat next and ask how many are left in the sea. The story ends with the shark eating them all.

"G" Sound: Explain to the children the difference between the hard **G** sound in words like **go** and the soft **G** sound in words like **giant**.

GA184

Language Arts Resources

Check resources for books, poems and films about **grandmothers, grandfathers, grocers, gardens, gray** squirrels, **ghosts, grammar, grapes, grasshoppers, groundhog, glasses** and **goldfish**.

Books:
George & the Cherry Tree, Aliki, Dial Press, 1964.
Georgie, Robert Bright, Doubleday, 1956.
The Gingerbread Man, Golden Press, 1973.
Three Billy Goats Gruff, Susan Blair (illust.), Holt, Rinehart, 1963.
Goldilocks and the Three Bears (see **T** week)

Films:
Big Green Caterpillar, Stanton Films.
Gray Squirrel, Encyclopedia Britannica Educational Corp.

Activities

Gruesome Mural: Early in the week begin to make a list of **gruesome** words that begin with the letter **G**, such as **gory, ghost, gorilla, garbage, guts, gash,** and **goop**, and don't forget **greasy, grimy** and **gopher**. Then have the children paint on **green** roll paper pictures to represent the words. Hang the mural up and attach label words.

Life-Size Gingerbread Boys: Children lie down on brown roll paper and trace each other in a simplified form representing a **gingerbread** cookie. Paint is applied in frosting-like decoration in white, pink and yellow.

Shades of Green: Discuss the difference in shadings of **green**. Use examples for several days. Include light **green**, Kelly **green**, dark **green**, chartreuse, etc. Duplicate shamrocks on various pieces of paper. Have the children cut them out and paste them on a background 9″ × 12″ sheet that has been titled "Shades of **Green**." (Shades of **gray** and **gold** can also be used for an exercise like this.)

Music

Songs:
Check song book indexes for **G** letter songs.

Records:
The following is a list of **G** letter songs found on Sesame Street Records: "Being Green," "Colors," "Garbage," "The Garden," "Giggles Goggles," "Grouch Song," "Patty Cake Gorilla" and "Two 'G' Sounds."

Science, Health and Social Studies

Gardens: Begin **gardening** or **gardening** experiments. Discuss different vegetables that are **grown** in **gardens** such as corn, **green** beans, radishes, onions, lettuce, cauliflower, potatoes and parsnips.

Grasshoppers: Walk outside to look for specimens to observe in the classroom. Check out books and films about **grasshoppers**.

Groundhogs: Another name for **groundhog** is woodchuck. Discuss its importance on **Groundhog** Day. Check resources for films and books about **groundhogs**.

Grains: Center a discussion around different grains **grown** in the United States. If possible, display some of these **grains**. The following are a few examples: wheat, corn, soybeans, barley, oats and rice.

Snacks

Serve the children **green** beans, **graham** crackers, **grapes**, **gum** drops, **grapefruit**, **gingerbread** or **ginger** snaps, **goldfish** crackers or **Gummi** Bears.

Special Fun

Grandparent's Day: Invite **grandparents** or older folks from the neighborhood for **gingerbread** or **gingerbread** cookies made by the class. Perhaps the visit could include sharing **G** songs and a short dramatization of the story "Gingerbread Man" or the Goldfish Counting Activity.

Evaluation and Testing

1. On **green** paper, draw four pictures of objects that start with the letter **G**.
2. Point to an upper case and a lower case **G** in print.
3. Speak to a friend using a **G** word.
4. Raise your hand when you hear me use a **G** word.
5. Give an example of **good** news.

GA184

71

The Sound of the Week is "A"

Timing

The best times for the sound of **A** are the first week in **April** or in the fall during the last week in September for **a** celebration of **Apple** Week and Johnny **Appleseed**'s birthday on September 26.

Special Environmental Considerations

Divide a bulletin board into long **A** and short **A** sections. Have the children bring in pictures **and** objects that begin with **A**. **As** they bring them in, have them help classify their **articles** into the right **A** section. When talking to the children, use responses such **as all** right, **a**-okay **and a**-ha.

Whole Language, Reading, and Math Readiness

Action Words: During the week, point out pictures that show **action** such **as** running, jumping, skipping, etc. Have the children identify the **action** words.

Alphabet Games: Many children **are** ready to think of the **alphabet** as a whole unit **and** respond well to common **alphabet** rhymes, songs **and** games (see Music section).

Apples: Compare, classify and group **apples** by color, size, number, circumference, weight, number of seeds, etc.

Alpha-Bits Cereal Activities: Give students portions of the cereal with which to do one or more of the following activities. Create more!

1. How many **A**'s are there in your portion?
2. Make a graph of the **A**'s in your portion.
3. Make an individual graph of the letters in your portion.
4. What letter did you have most frequently?
5. Make your name.
6. Make one or more other words from your portion.

Language Arts Resources

Books:

April Fool, Leland Jacobs, Champaign, Illinois, Garrard Publishing Company, 1973.

April's Kittens, Newberry, Harper, 1940.

Attic of the Wind, Lund, Parents Magazine Press, 1966.

GA184

Poetry:

Two little apples hanging from a tree
  (fists in air)

Two little apples looking at me.
  (turn fists inward)

I shook the tree as hard as I could
  (shake fists)

Down came the apples!
  (fists down)

My! They were good!
  (rub tummy)

    Traditional Author Unknown

Activities

Aprons: This project makes a useful gift to save for Mother's Day. Each child needs several paper place mats **and a** yard of ribbon. The ribbon is sewn **along** the long side of the stack of place mats to make **an apron.** The top place mat can be torn off **as** it becomes soiled.

American Flag: Children paste 1″ × 18″ red strips on white 12″ × 18″ paper. **A** blue 6″ × 9″ field is **applied** to the top **at** the left corner. Indicate that **any** number of stars from 13 to 50 is correct. The Old Glory **arrangement** of 13 stars in **a** circle seems the easiest for young children.

Music

Songs:

The song book *Music for Young Americans* has the songs "Abraham Lincoln" **and** "Five Little Alligators." In the book *Making Music Your Own,* by Mary T. Jaye **and** Imogene Hilyard, is the song "Allee Allee O!" The song book *The American Singer, Book I,* by John Beattle, has the song "April." Learn "America" and "America the Beautiful" and "Mockingbird Flight."

Records:

Sesame Street Records has the songs "AB-C-DEF-GHI," "Adding," "Roosevelt Franklin's Alphabet" and "Sound of the Letter A." "Alphabet March" is from the album *Learning Basic Skills, Vol. 1.*

GA184

Health, Science and Social Studies

Air: Introduce the following concepts to the class.

Concept: Air is found in many places.

> Pour water into **a** transparent container.
> Blow up **a** balloon **and** hold the neck.
> Put the balloon into the water.
> Slowly let the **air** out.

> Put **a** rock into the water.
> Watch for bubbles.
> **Air** is in the rock.

Concept: Air expands.

> Place a balloon over the neck of **a** small bottle half full of hot water.
> Place the bottle in **a** pan of boiling water.
> **As** water **and air** get hotter, the balloon will inflate.

Concept: Air contains oxygen.

> Set **a** candle in **a** large jar **and** light it.
> Place the lid on the jar.
> When the oxygen has burned, the flame will go out.
> **Caution:** The lid will be hot; take care when removing it.

Ants: Provide opportunities to observe **and** discuss information centered **around ants**. Set up **an ant** farm.

Snacks

Make **applesauce** in class.

Serve the children **apples, apricots, asparagus, artichokes, avocados, angel** food cake, **almonds, Alpha-Bits** cereal or **alphabet** macaroni (soup).

Evaluation and Testing

1. Given **an A** word, identify whether it has **a** long or short **A** sound.
2. Name **a** food that begins with **A.**
3. Identify the letter **A** in print.

GA184

BOYS
black
blue
brown

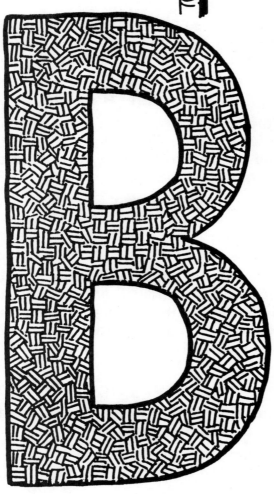

75

The Sound of the Week is "B"

Timing

An excellent time to present the **B** is in the spring of the year near Easter. Emphasis can be placed on **bunnies**, **babies** and **birds**.

Special Environmental Considerations

Provide **books** and prints that show a variety of **bunnies, baby** animals and **birds**. This should help diminish the stereotype that all **bunnies** are white, all **birds** are robins and all **baby** animals are just miniature versions of the adult species. When talking to the children, use positive **B** letter words such as **bright**, **beautiful**, and **better**.

Whole Language, Reading, and Math Readiness

Coloring by Key: Provide duplicated drawings of **B** objects in which numbers on the areas to be colored are keyed to a color word list. Observe which children can correlate the numbers and colors.

Black, Blue and Brown: One day limit paints to these colors. Allow play with only these colored components of toys. Designate a day to wear and share and eat things that are each of the **B** colors.

Bouncing: Practice **bouncing** and catching a **ball both** individually and to another person. **By** the end of kindergarten, the children should **be** able to catch a **ball bounced** to them without squatting and without always having it hit them in the chin.

Language Arts Resources

Check the library for books, poems and films about **birds, babies, brothers, balls** and **big**.

Books:

B Book, Berenstein, NY: Random House, 1971.

The Country Bunny and the Little Gold Shoes, Heyward, NY: Houghton Mifflin, 1939.

The Easter Bunny That Overslept, Friedrich, NY: Lothrop, Lee, Shephard, 1969.

Home For a Bunny, Margaret Wise Brown, Racine, Wisconsin: Golden Press, 1956.

My "B" Sound Box, Jane Moncure, Chicago: Children's Press, 1977.

GA184

Poetry:

Bunny Handplay

Here's a bunny with ears so funny
(raise two fingers)

Here's his hole in the ground
(circle thumb and index finger)

When a noise he hears

He pricks up his ears,
(wiggle "ear" fingers)

And jumps in his hole in the ground
(ears into the circle made by thumb
and index finger)

Some other possible **B** letter poems can **be** found in Shel Silverstein's **book** *Where the Sidewalk Ends.* They are "Bagpipe Who Didn't Say No," "Band-aids" and "Boa Constrictor."

Activities

Blot Print Butterflies: The teacher traces a **butterfly** outline on a 12" × 18" piece of construction paper. The children cut out the **butterfly** and drip paint on one side. The paper is folded, pressed together and then opened to reveal a print that is the same on **both** wings. The process may **be** repeated on the other side after the first side has dried.

Tissue Blossom Trees: Have the children draw or paint a **bare** tree on 12" × 18" paper. Circles of pink napkins or tissue are applied to dabs of paste or are glued onto the **branches**. A little pinch given to the centers of the circles gives the **blossoms** a more realistic appearance.

Sponge-Painted Blossoms: The children draw or paint a **bare** tree on 12" × 18" construction paper. **Blossoms** are sponge-painted on in pink.

Love Bunny: Prepare a master of the **bunny** parts, as shown in the illustration **below**, for the total **bunny**. Have the children cut out the different pieces and assemble them. Thin strips of scraps can be used to make the whiskers. A cotton **ball** is applied for a tail.

77

GA184

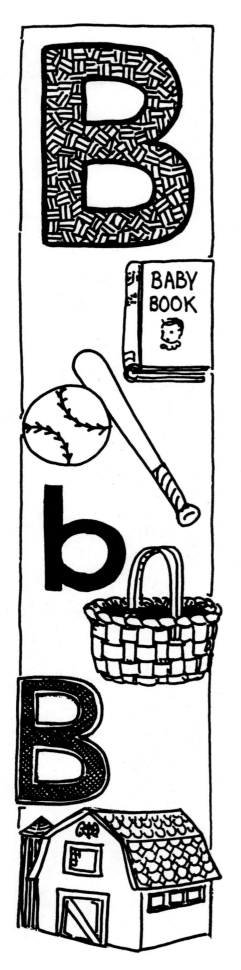

Bunny Masks: Have the children cut out ears from 4" × 12" construction paper and attach them to a paper plate in which eyes have **been** cut. A Popsicle stick is attached for the handle. Pieces of Strofoam packing material can **be** glued on if available. (See illustration for completed **bunny** masks.)

Bert's Big B Sandwich: Listen to the song "B Sandwich" found on Sesame Street Records *Let a Frown Be Your Umbrella*. Let the children select a sandwich ingredient to paint and cut out. Then have them stack up their ingredients like a sandwich to dramatize the song.

Beanbag Activities: Beanbags can be made by the children using Styrofoam packing material and Zip-loc bags or by sewing 4" scrap squares of material with yarn. Making the **beanbags** and related activities can assist the children in developing coordination, fitness and hand-eye coordination. Challenges can include tossing the **bags** to each other or into containers and moving with the **bag balanced** on their instep or head. Try to involve different **body** parts and positions as much as possible. Use the record *Bean Bag Activities*, Kimbo Educational Records, Long Branch, NJ 07740.

Music

Songs:
A few **B** letter songs can **be** found in the **book** *Music for Young Americans* by Richard Berg. They are "Horn on the Bus," "I Like a Bike," "School Bus" and "The Bear Went Over the Mountain." Another **B** letter song is "The Bluebird," found in the **book** *Small Songs for Small Singers* by W. H. Neidlinger.

Special Note: Some possible subjects for **B** letter songs are **babies, balls, bears, bees, bikes, birds, blue, bugs, bunnies** and **buses**.

GA184

Science, Health and Social Studies

Birds: Assemble **bird** nests and enlarge prints of eggs and **birds** for observation and comparison. Perhaps the children would enjoy going on a **bird** walk. How many different **birds** can they see?

Bees and Bugs: The children's interests might **be best** served in observation and comparison similar to the **bird** study.

Bunnies: Observe and compare **bunnies** in relation to **birds** and **bugs**. Develop the concept of animal families. A **bunny** is an easy animal to have visit the classroom if someone has one to **bring**.

Bones: Obtain old x-rays from a local doctor. Ask for x-ray examples of whole **bones** and **broken bones** that have healed. Try to obtain enough x-rays to assemble a complete figure. Or, if possible, use a skeleton. Contrasting adult and children's **bones** can be interesting.

Buckle Up: Most state and local law enforcement agencies have free or inexpensive materials that promote use of seat belts.

Snacks

Serve the children **bread, butter, biscuits, butterscotch** (candy or pudding), **bologna, bananas** and **berries**.

Special Fun

Breakfast in School: Having **breakfast** in school is one way to allow the children to dye eggs without having to store them until Easter. Each child **brings** two hard-**boiled** eggs to school on Thursday. They are dyed that day. Invite an upper grade class to hide the eggs on Friday. Then have the children hunt for their eggs. Once the eggs are found, **breakfast** is ready to **be** served. This would include **bananas**, milk, hot cross or other **buns** or **biscuits**, and the found eggs. **Breakfast** is completed with hot cross **buns**. For a variation of this idea, invite the class that hid the eggs to join your **Breakfast** Party.

Invite a **baker** to visit. Perhaps he could **bring** the hot cross **buns** for the **breakfast** or demonstrate how to **bake biscuits**.

Invite the school **band** to play for your class. Or, ask if the class can visit a school **band** practice.

79

GA184

Practice **bus** emergency procedures. This is especially important if the class comes to school by **bus**. Invite the **bus** driver in for snack time or take him a treat in appreciation for his work.

Ask the children to **bring** their **baby** pictures from home. Display the pictures and have the children try to guess who's who.

Boat Show: Encourage children to bring toy **boats** to show, tell about, and test-float if possible. Create **boats** from scraps of wood or even folded paper and have a show or regatta. Use the collection to count, size, graph, classify, order from largest to smallest, etc.

Evaluation and Testing

1. Sing "The Bear Went Over the Mountain," which is found in the book *Music for Young Americans.* Have the children name one **B** object that the **bear** might have seen as he crossed over the mountain.
2. Identify the letter **B** in print.
3. Give a **boy's** name that starts with the letter **B**.
4. Name **B** things that people might find if they visited a grocery store, a clothing store, the woods, a zoo, a **ball** diamond or a **baby**.

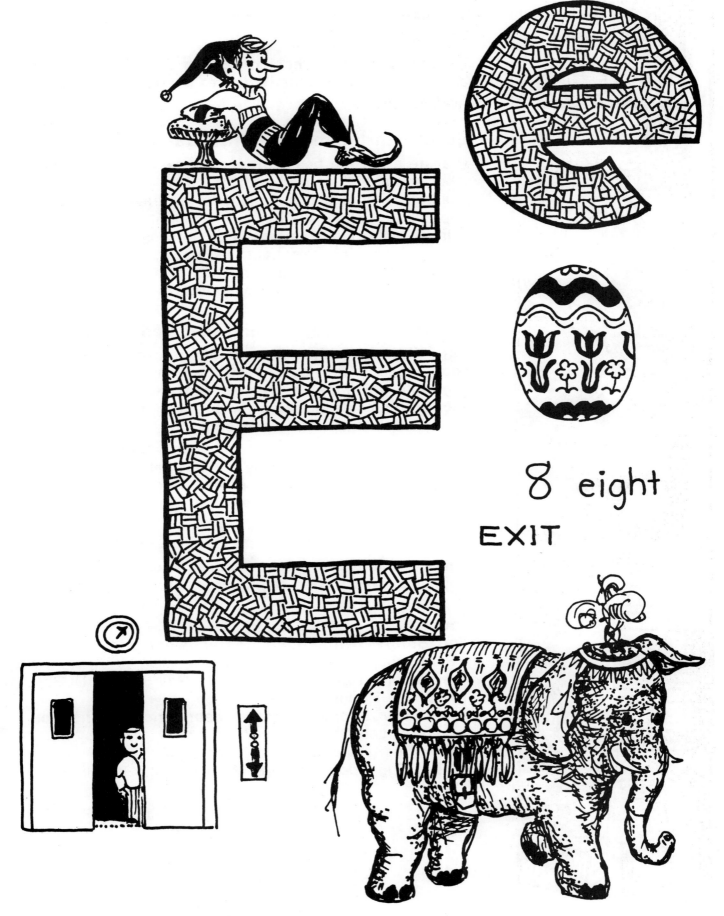

8 eight

EXIT

81

The Sound of the Week Is "E"

Timing

By scheduling this letter before **Easter**, E week can be billed as an **egg event** if holiday activities are discouraged in the local schools.

Special Environmental Considerations

Prepare a bulletin board divider for the sound board and label one side "Long **E**" and the other "Short **E**." As the children bring objects and pictures, separate them into the appropriate columns. Objects that might be included on a label table might be: **envelope, encyclopedia, earring, eraser, eggs, eight, elephant, elk, eagle, eskimo** and **ear**. Objects in the room to label might include: **easel, exercise equipment, eight, eleven, encyclopedia** and **elbow**.

Whole Language, Reading, and Math Readiness

Egg Math Activities: Secure **egg** cartons in several configurations. Provide at least a dozen plastic or blown **eggs** with which the children can **experiment** to prove that **each** carton holds the same number of **eggs**. Also compare the different sizes of the blown **eggs**.

Visual Discrimination: Collect and post pictures of **ears** and **eyes**. Have the children guess who or what the **ears** or **eyes** belong to. Include human, animal, and corn **ears**, and human, animal and potato **eyes**.

Language Arts Resources

Check the library for books, films and poems about **eggs, elephants, eyes, Easter, earthquakes** and **electricity**.

Books:
The Bunny Who Found Easter, Charlotte Zolotow, Parnassus, 1959.
The Country Bunny and the Little Gold Shoes, DuBose Heyward, Houghton, 1939.
The Easter Bunny That Overslept, Priscilla Friedrich, Lothrop, Lee, Shepard, 1957.
Easter Treat, Roger Duvoisin, Knopf, 1954.
Golden Egg Book, Margaret Wise Brown, Golden Press, 1962.

GA184

Poetry:

I Can Write!
I make an M and I make an E
They spell a word and the word is "Me."
It's the first I've learned; it sure is fun!
I think I'll show it to everyone!

Activities

Bunny Ear Headbands: Have the children make a headband from a strip of 4" × 24" paper and attach bunny **ears** to it. These can be worn throughout the week for different activities.

Pastel Eggs: Give the children 9" × 12" sheets of paper with an **egg** outline on **each**. Allow them to color the **eggs** using colored chalks. Demonstrate how to fill in the background color by rubbing with the side of the chalk and then how to add detail with the **end** of the chalk. Hair spray applied to the finished **eggs** retards smearing. Washing the sheets with liquid starch, applied with a sponge before drawing, prevents some smearing.
(Make sure the children have smocks or aprons to wear.)

Graph Paper Eggs: Children can have **experience** in repeating the design if they color the squares in **eggs** that have been duplicated on 1" graph paper.

Tissue Overlay: Interesting **effects** and **experimentation** with mixing colors can take place when plain white **eggs** are brushed with liquid starch and then scraps of colored tissue paper are applied in overlapping patterns.

Eskimo: Have the children fold 9" × 12" paper in half and trace their hands, mitten style. Cut out the mittens. Then cut a circle from a 4" square for a face. Apply paste around the **edge** of the face and trim it with cotton for effect. Attach the head to the mittens and draw facial features (see illustration).

Stand-up Elephant: (see illustration, p. 105) Fold 9" × 12" gray paper to form a 6" × 4½" rectangle. Cut a half-circle from the open **edges**. Clip on the fold to make a slot

for the head. Cut a circle from a 4½" square of gray paper for the head. Add a 1" × 4" strip for the trunk. Trim the half-circle scraps for **ears** and a tail. Add **eyes** if desired.

Music

Songs:
The song book *My Picture Book of Songs* by Alene Dalton has the songs "Easter Morning" and "Jumbo." And *The American Singer, Book I*, by John Beattle, has the song "I Am Bunny Pink Ears."

Records: Little Golden Records has the song "Easter Parade." And Sesame Street Records has the songs "Silent E" and "I Want to Hold Your Ears."

Special Note: Check sources for songs about **Easter** bunnies, **eagles, elk, elephants** and **exercises**.

Science, Health and Social Studies

Eggs: Amplify the study of **eggs** by **exploring** their shape and color for adaptation to various bird habitats.

Earthquakes: If you live in an earthquake area this is a good time to practice **earthquake** drills.

Electricity: Most local utilities offer materials to teach and promote **electrical** safety.

Snacks

Some possible **E** letter snacks are **eggs, English** muffins, **eggnog, enchiladas, egg** rolls and **eclairs**.

Special Fun

Invite an **electrician** to visit the class and discuss the positive and negative aspects of **electricity**.

Invite an **energy** specialist to discuss different ways to conserve **energy**.

Evaluation and Testing

1. Name two things that begin with the long **E** sound and two things that begin with the short **E** sound.
2. Put **eight E** pictures into an **envelope**.
3. Identify upper and lower case **E** in print.

GA184

The Sound of the Week is "D"

Timing

Schedule the letter **D** in the spring for focus on **ducks, daffodils** and **dandelions**. Or, another possibility is to schedule it sometime **during** the month of **December**.

Special Environmental Considerations

Give all the girls name tags for **daughters**. **Display** Walt **Disney** cartoon characters throughout the room.

Whole Language, Reading, and Math Readiness

Directions: Review the **directions** of left and right (see **L** week). Kindergartners should be able to carry out three-step **directions** once they've been given. **During** the early part of the week, two-step **directions** could be given to get the children accustomed to the procedure and to **develop** their confidence. By the end of the week they should be able to handle three **directions** given at one time, such as:

1. Go to the chalkboard; **draw** a line and erase it.
2. Go to the **door**; open it, then close it.
3. Stand up straight; skip to the light switch, then touch it.
4. Touch your toes; touch your knees; touch your hair.
5. Stand up; touch your toes and touch your ears.
6. Touch your shoulders; touch your nose; jump up.
7. Jump up; sit **down** and cross your legs.
8. Point to the window; pick up a book and put it on a chair.
9. Pick up a pencil; hold it over your **desk**, then **drop** it.
10. Skip to the **door**; skip to the window and jump to your chair.
11. Go to the pencil sharpener; turn the handle two times; clap your hands.
12. Show me a red crayon; pick up a pencil and point to a blue crayon.
13. Stand on one foot; hop three times; turn around.
14. Close your eyes; cover your ears; stick out your tongue.
15. Close one eye; clap your hands; nod your head.
16. Clap your hands behind you, then in front, then above your head.
17. Jump three times; hop twice on each foot.
18. Shake a boy's hand; pat a girl on the back; clap three times.

GA184

19. Blink your eyes; shake your head; cross your fingers.
20. Turn left; turn around the opposite way; walk backwards three steps.

Dice Race: This works better with **dice** made from cubes such as truffles boxes, cut down milk cartons, foam cubes or other square boxes. Two or three children line up at a starting point and, in turn, **drop** the **dice** and move that many spaces (spaces could be squares of vinyl floor tile, cards, etc.). To control throwing, each child must reach **down** and pick up the **dice** for the next turn. If the **dice** is too far away, the child must start over. The first one to goal wins.

Dice Designs: Provide children with **dice** and papers on which the numerals 1-6 are scattered and repeated several times for each numeral. The child rolls the **dice**, puts a mark on the numeral that comes up, rolls again, marks that numeral, etc. Rolls continue until all the numerals are used. The child then makes the **design** into a figure or colors in the spaces to make a **design**.

Dice Recording: Have children roll one **dice** and graph the results. Talk about probability. This can be done as a group or individual project.

Dominoes: Introduce several types of **domino** games as available. Use both picture and symbol **dominoes** as well as the traditional type. The ability to play a game with another child or in a small group **demonstrates** a maturing of socialization skills above the parallel play of the younger child.

Dime: Work with coins to **develop** the concept of the value of a **dime**. Also work with the **dollar**.

Diamonds: Develop awareness of rhomboids by finding samples of **diamond**-shaped things.

Dozen: Discuss the meaning of the term **dozen**. If possible, have egg cartons in the 3″ × 4″ and 6″ × 2″ configurations and blown egg shells for manipulation proof. What is a baker's **dozen**?

Language Arts Resources

Check sources for books, poems and films about **dinosaurs, ducks, dogs, Dads, deer, drugs,** and **dragons.**

Books:
Dinosaurs, Kathryn Jackson, National Geographic Society, 1972.
Danny and the Dinosaur, Sydney Hoff, Harper, 1958.
Dead Tree, Alvin Tresselt, Parents Magazine Press, 1972.

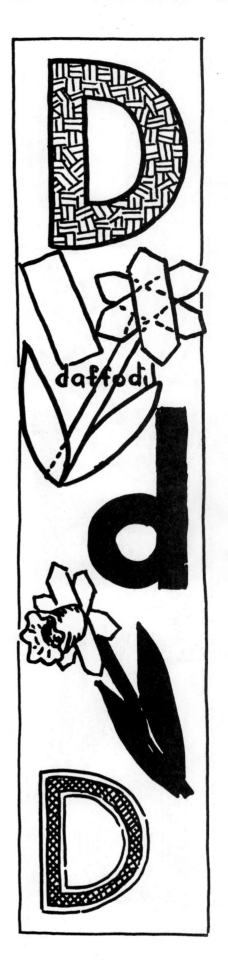

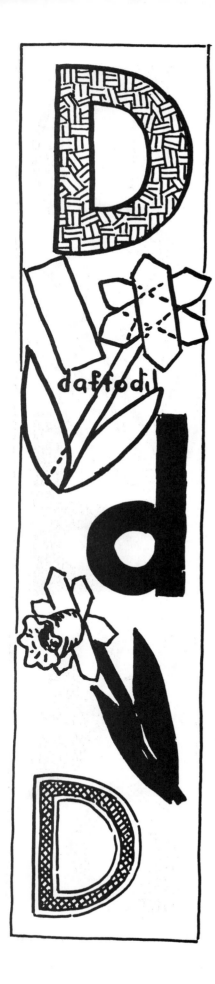

Dragon in the Clock Box, Jean Craig, Grosset & Dunlop, NY, 1962.

Ducks Don't Get Wet, Kessler, Crowell, NY, 1965.

Make Way for Ducklings, Robert McCloskey, Viking, 1941.

Activities

D Mural: Define the word "mural" for the children. **Develop** an area of sky, ground and water for a mural background. This might be accomplished by cutting roll paper of blues and greens, or by sponging and then painting large areas of blues and greens on white paper. The children then paint separate pictures of **ducks, daffodils, dogs, dandelions** and other **D** objects. Cut out the pictures and attach them to the mural. Label the objects after they are included in the group painting.

Dot Dragons: Give students sheets of paper on which they put a **dozen dots** at random. They then connect the **dots** in any order and then try to form some kind of fantastic **dragon** or **dinosaur** from the shape. Encourage using a typical skin covering and appendages and even giving the creature a name.

Donuts: Give each child a **duplicated donut** shape or let each free-cut a **donut**. Paint with pink, white or brown tempera to which a little white glue has been added. While the paint is wet, sprinkle it with fine shreds of paper (for coconut) or punch dots.

Dad: Have the children **draw** pictures of their **Dads**.

Daffodils: Make a simple **daffodil** by crossing 3 1" × 4" pointed yellow strips to make a star shape for petals. Form the trumpet with a tube of 3" wide crepe paper or yellow tissue paper. Add stems and leaves.

Origami Dog: Fold a square of paper **diagonally** to form a triangle. Fold the points at each end of the fold forward and **down** to form the head and ears. Add features. The head may be attached to a stand-up body by folding another sheet (9" × 12") into fourths, cutting away half-circles to form the legs and placing the head in a slit cut in the fold of the back. Trim a scrap of the half-circle for a tail (see stand-up animals, page 105).

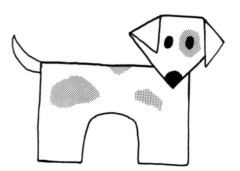

88

Music

Songs:
"Darling Clementine" is a favorite children's song. Also, *My Picture Book of Songs*, by Alene Dalton, has the song "Dog Songs."

Records:
Burl Ives has recorded the songs "Watch the Donut, Not the Hole" and "Little White Duck" for Columbia Records. Sesame Street Records has the songs "Dee, Dee, Dee" and "Up & Down" to offer, while *The Ballad of Lucy Lum*, Good Apple, Inc., has "Don't Burn Down the Birthday Cake." Another song the children will enjoy is "Puff, the Magic Dragon," published by Golden Records.

Rhythms:
Use available resources to respond rhythmically as **dolls, dragons, ducks, dogs,** and **deer. Dancing** and **drums** can also be incorporated in the activities.

Science, Health and Social Studies

Doctor and Dentist: Arrange a visit to a **doctor's** or **dentist's** office. **Discuss** the **different** "tools" used by **dentists** and **doctors**.

Ducks: A visiting **duck** or **duckling** would be enjoyed by the children in the class. Or, an excursion to feed the **ducks** can stimulate **discussion** and will aid the mural activities **described** earlier in the activity section.

Dreams: Allow time for each child to share a **dream** he/she has had. **Discuss** feelings and possible reasons for **dreams**. Focus on allaying fears.

Drugs: This is a good time to discuss substance abuse. Check the library and drug agencies for materials.

Snacks

Serve delicious snacks such as **dates, dried** fruit, **devil's** food cake, **Dr.** Pepper and **dandelion dip**.

Dandelion Dip
Mix in a blender until spreadable:
1 cup new, washed **dandelion** leaves (from plants not bloomed)
½ cup cottage cheese
¼ cup nuts
Enough mayonnaise to achieve consistency. Spread on crackers to serve.

GA184

Special Fun

Dog Show: A **dog** show can be a rewarding and sharing experience if carefully planned and controlled. All **dogs** must be accompanied by an adult and be kept on a leash. Have the show outside. Award ribbons for appropriate categories. Have the adults take the **dogs** home when the show is over. Or have a toy dog show or bring photos of family **dogs**. Allow time for sharing.

Dad's Day: Invite the children's fathers to visit the class. Serve **devil's** food cake and **Dr.** Pepper. If possible, give each father a **daisy** boutonniere. The children will enjoy making these for the **Dads**.

Evaluation and Testing

1. Respond correctly to a three-step **direction**.
2. Name four things that start with the letter **D**.
3. **Dramatize** something that starts with the letter **D**.
4. Identify both the upper and lower case **D** in print.
5. Identify a **dime** and a **dollar**.
6. Count out a **dozen** objects.

GA184

GA184

The Sound of the Week is "H"

Timing

The sound of **H** can fit anywhere in the program. **H** is an easy sound for the children to understand. **H** can also be presented around **Halloween** or one of the **holidays.**

Special Environmental Considerations

Emphasize verbal manners and greetings such as **Hello, How** are you, **Hi**, and **Howdy**.

Whole Language, Reading and Math Readiness

Classifying H Objects: During discussion, **have** the children identify different objects that begin with the letter **H.** Some of these could be things to eat, wear, different feelings, body parts and animals. This activity can be continued with subsequent sounds, too.

Hundred Hearts: Have children bring or wear things with **hearts** to school. Keep track on a graph (with a **heart** stamp or stickers) in rows of tens to see if they can find a **hundred** or more!

Collect and try to decipher "I ♡ ____" buttons and stickers.

Conceptualizing with the Letter H: Play guessing games in which the students try to identify objects in the room with clues such as: It is **high, hard, heavy, hot** or **handy.**

Height: Develop this concept by recording and comparing **heights** of things in the room.

Language Arts Resources

Check resources for books, poems and films about **hats, hippos, happy** stories, **hospital, health, hand, houses, homes, hamsters.**

Books:
Attic of the Wind, Doris Lund, Parents Magazine Press, 1966.
Belinda's New Spring Hat, Clymer, F. Watts Co., 1969.
Happy Lion, Fatio, McGraw Hill, 1954.
Little Red Hen, Begley, Golden Press, 1966.
My H Sound Box, Jane Moncure, Children's Press, 1977.

GA184

Poetry:

Hippety-Hop

Hippety Hop came hopping by,
Hippety-hippety-hop.

He wiggled an ear and he winked an eye,
Hippety-hippety-hop.

He hopped in the meadow; he hopped on the hill,
Hippety-hippety-hop.

For all I know, he's hopping still,
Hippety-hippety-hop.

Hippos

Hippos are round
and go at a trot
They never gallop
They sleep a lot.

They can't do tricks
Like the bears and the seals
But they're all of them
Very prompt at meals!

My Hands

I have hands that teach me.

They help me learn a lot.
They tell me if the things I touch
Are cold or warm or hot.

I know round and I know square.
I can tell them anywhere.
I know smooth and I know rough.
Hard and soft? That's not so tough!

When I'm finished pasting
My fingers feel so sticky
But fingerpainting's best of all
Because it feels so icky!

D. Heckerling

Activities

Hand Painting: Focus on the concept of **hand** painting rather than finger painting and use this art form to include the entire **hand** rather than just the fingertips.

Hoops: These can be purchased, or made by coupling 30 inches of **half**-inch flexible plastic pipe with a dowel and staples or manufactured nylon couplers. Activities can include movement activities inside, outside, over, under and through the **hoops**.

93

GA184

Houses: Each child needs a shoe box and construction paper for the ends of the **house**. Duplicate outlines of a telephone, birthday cake, mother, father, brother, sister, baby and **heart** on a sheet of paper. **Have** the children cut out the shapes and put them in their **houses**. On the appropriate shape write the child's telephone number, address, birthdate and names of family members as provided by the child. The **heart** can **have** written on it something that makes the **home** a **happy** place for the child.

Hyacinths: Paper representations of these flowers can be made by pasting crushed pieces of colored tissue to a stem. These can be adapted to a Mother's Day card by scenting the paper with powder or cologne.

Horseshoes: If possible, teach the children **how** to play the game of **horseshoes**.

Hand Art: Have children trace their **hands** to make figures such as flowers or swans, or just a collage of crayoned or cut-out **hands**.

Hats: Use imagination to make **hats** from sacks, paper plates, newspaper and other odds and ends.

Music

Songs:
The songs "Hey Diddle Diddle," "The Little Red Hen," and "Humpty Dumpty" can be found in *The Kindergarten Book*, by Lilla Belle Pitts. "I Can't Spell Hippopotamus" is found in *Mockingbird Flight.*

Records:
Sesame Street Records has the songs "Ha Ha," "High, Middle and Low," "Hello", and "Hard, Hard, Hard."

Science, Health and Social Studies

H Body Parts: Identify body parts that begin with the letter **H**. The following is a list: **hair, head, hands, hips, heart** and **heel**. Play response games such as "Simon Says" using the **H** parts.

Hampsters: If any of the children **have** pet **hamsters**, invite them to bring their pets to class. If possible, observe and care for some **hamsters**. See films and read stories about them.

Health Emphasis: Discuss the importance of being **healthy**. **Health** is more than just physical; it also deals with mental adjustments, social adjustments, religious adjustments, etc. Being **healthy** is something that money can't buy. Stress the importance of each individual being concerned about his/her own **health**. This should be an active concern.

Half: Develop this concept by dividing groups, materials and snacks in **half**.

Snacks

Ham, honey, hot dogs, **hamburgers,** and **Hawaiian** Punch can be served for snacks.

Another possibility is to make **Heavenly Hash** or **Haystack** Cookies in the room.

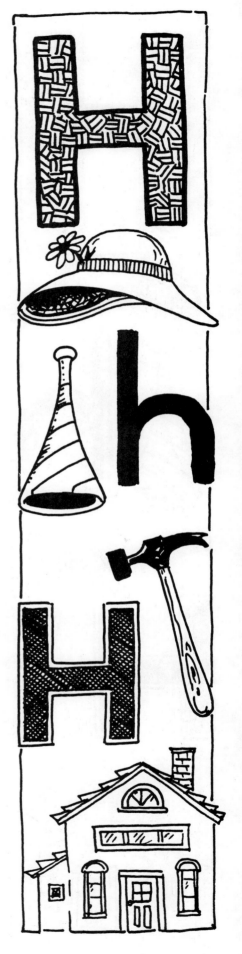

Heavenly Hash

2 cups drained pineapple tidbits
2 cups drained mandarin orange sections
1 cup diced maraschino cherries
1 cup shredded coconut
1 cup sour cream
1 bag miniature marsh-mallows

Allow to stand one **hour** or more so flavors blend.

Haystack Cookies
(Makes about 24)
Melt: 12 oz. chocolate chips
or 6 oz. chocolate and 6 oz. butterscotch bits
Add: 1 cup peanuts or peanut butter
Stir in one can of Chinese noodles. Mix and drop from spoon onto waxed paper to cool.

Special Fun

Arrange to Visit a Hospital: Many **hospitals** are **happy** to introduce children to their facilities in a relaxed, non-stressful class visit.

Hat Day: Select a day when the children may bring or wear a favorite or interesting **hat**. Allow time for sharing and discussion.

Hawaii: The children may enjoy discussion and sharing about our 50th state. Play **Hawaiian** music. Display ukuleles, **Hawaiian** dress, leis and different foods. Discuss the culture and the tropical **habitat**.

Hobby Day: Invite the children to bring all or part of their **hobby** collections to class. **Have** a show-and-tell **hour**.

Harmonicas and Horns: Invite a person who plays the **harmonica** or a **horn** instrument to play for the class. If this is not possible, play records with **harmonica** and **horn** music. Have children bring **horns** or **harmonicas** if they **have** them and play along.

Evaluation and Testing

1. Name something that begins with **H** that could be bought at a food store, clothing store, pet store, etc.

GA184

2. **Have** the children pretend that they are going to visit a doctor. **Have** them greet the doctor and explain a problem they are **having** with an **H** part of their body.

3. Identify the upper and lower case letter **H** in print.

Extended H Activities

Harbor: If there is a **harbor** near the location of the school, take the children to visit. Discuss different things that can be found at a **harbor** such as boats, sailors and seagulls.

Hen Eggs: If possible, find an incubator. Get fertilized eggs and place them in the incubator. The children will enjoy waiting for the chicks to **hatch** and observing their growth after they **have hatched**.

Hobo Day: Declare a **Hobo** Day and invite the children to dress as **hobos**. They will enjoy **hobo** stories and discussing a **hobo's** life.

GA184

97

The Sound of the Week is "M"

Timing

A natural time to present the letter **M** is during the **month** of **May** around **Mother's** Day. Another possibility is one week during the **month** of **March**.

Special Environmental Considerations

A bulletin board of people and animals with their young could be displayed. Label cards with the word "**mother**" on them could be attached to the **mothers** in the pictures. Also **make** label cards for the **males** in the class.

Whole Language, Reading and Math Readiness

Maps: Prepare a **map** of the school neighborhood. Identify places of interest. Plan a walk that will involve using the **map**. Have other **maps** available for inspection, such as town, state, road, wilderness, U.S., world and **moon maps**. A variation of this is to **make** a treasure **map** of the playground and hide the buried treasure somewhere there. Let the children try to find the treasure by following directions and using the **map**.

M & M's Math: M & M's lend themselves perfectly to counting, classifying, graphing and **making** patterns.

Measurement: Provide a selection of **measures**, both **metric** and English, for experimentation and **manipulation**. **Make** sure the children have a chance to use rulers, yardsticks, and **metric** sticks for **measuring**. **Marshmallows make** good units with which to **measure** things.

Money: This is a good week to focus on the value of coins. An extension of simple recognition is to provide cards with coins traced on them that add up to 25¢ in several ways, such as 25 pennies, two dimes and a nickel, five nickels, etc. Another possibility is to introduce the use of bills.

Many, Much, More: Discuss these terms with the children. These concepts can be introduced with the song "How Many Mannies," from *Imagination & Me*, Good Apple, Inc.

Me, My, Mine: Discuss concepts dealing with these words. **Make** sure the children have practice using each one correctly.

GA184

Language Arts Resources

Check resources for books, poems and movies about **magnets, mountains, Mother, mice,** and **manners**.

Books:
A Map Is a Picture, Barbara Rinkoff, Crowell, 1962.
How Big Is a Foot, Rolf Myller, Atheneum Pub., 1962.
Mickey's Magnet, Franklyn Branley, Crowell, 1956.
Mousekin, (Series), Edna Miller, Prentice Hall, 1967ff.
Mud, Mud, Mud, Lenore Klein, Knopf, 1962.

Activities

Mother's Day Card: The child's handprint on a card with a **Mother's** Day poem **makes** an effective and appreciated **memento**.

> Dear Mother,
> This will help you to remember
> When I've grown big and tall,
> That once I was quite little and
> My hand was very small.
> So, for Mother's Day,
> I'm giving this you see,
> With a tiny note that says,
> "Much love, to you, from me."

Mud Finger Painting: This activity can be done with several different **media**. The children can finger paint with real **mud** if it is available. Instant chocolate pudding **makes** a **mud**-like substance that is fun to lick off after the painting is finished. Of course, brown paint can always be used. Attach the following verse to the painting.

> **Mud** is very nice to feel
> All squish-squash between the toes!
> I'd rather wade in wiggly **mud**
> Than smell a yellow rose.
>
> Nobody else but the rosebush knows
> How nice **mud** feels
> Between the toes.

Polly Chase Boyden

Magic Pictures: Place a piece of waxed paper over a piece of white paper. Have the children draw with a pencil or stick on the waxed paper. Put a watercolor wash on the white paper and the drawing on the waxed paper will appear. Or, draw on white paper with lemon juice and a cotton swab. Iron the paper or place it in a hot oven. The drawing will appear.

GA184

Monsters: Allow the children to invade the scrap and junk boxes to create imaginary creatures of their own design. Encourage verbalization by having each child share his/her **monster** with the class.

Movement Activities: These provide the children with experience in exploring how their bodies **move** in space. Exercises **might** include stretching, curling up, twisting, balancing, weight transfer, changing directions, over and under, and lifting and lowering, as well as the **more** common running, jumping, hopping, skipping, galloping, etc.

Mural: Have the children design a wall **mural**. Hang brown paper, similar to white butcher paper, on the wall. Then let the children draw, paint and color a **musical mural**, a **machine mural** or a **mosaic mural**.

Sack Mouse: Each child will need a lunch-size sack and a sheet of newspaper. Draw a line on the sack about 2½″ from the open end and cut the end off of the sack on the line. Crumple newspaper and stuff the remaining sack. Fold the top corner of the open end down to the side of the sack and staple it (see figure 1). From the cut off piece of sack, cut a thin strip for a tail and two ears. Pleat the ears and staple or glue them on both sides of the head. Add eyes, nose and strips for whiskers (see sample).

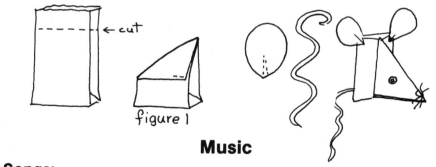

figure 1

Music

Songs:

In the Merry Month of May

In the merry month of May, All the world seems bright and gay, Ba-by leaves come out to play, In the merry month of May.

Maypole Dance

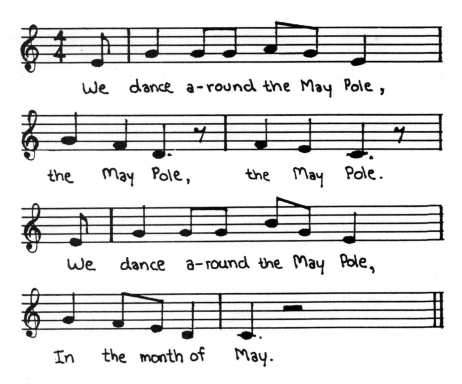

We dance a-round the May Pole,
the May Pole, the May Pole.
We dance a-round the May Pole,
In the month of May.

Verses: 2. Let's all bow to the **May** Pole, etc.
3. Girls in to the **May** Pole, etc.
4. Boys around the **May** Pole, etc.
5. Boys in to the **May** Pole, etc.
6. Girls around the **May** Pole, etc.
7. All go 'round the **May** Pole, etc.

Special Note: Check sources for **marching** songs and a **medley** of songs.

Science, Health and Social Studies

Magnets: Provide a collection of various types and powers of **magnets**. Set up some of the experiments described in primary books on **magnetism**. Be sure to include *Mickey's Magnet* (see book section). **Make magnets** from pins as shown in the book.

Magnifiers and Mirrors: Make available for **manipulation** and exploration.

Marigold: Plant **marigolds** in containers for **Mother's** Day.

GA184

Snacks

Make muffins from a **mix** or use **measurement** activities to **make muffins**.

Marshmallows, mints, milk, macaroons, macaroni, maple, melon, molasses, mushrooms, marmalade and **M & M**'s are a few possibilities for **meal** time.

Special Fun

Arrange for a visit from the **mailman** or a **magician** or the town **mayor**.

Plan a **Mother's** Tea. Have the children invite their **mothers**. Serve **milk, macaroons** and **mints**.

If possible, go for a **merry**-go-round ride. Use **money** activities in purchasing tickets.

Show the children how to play **marbles**.

If there is interest, develop activities about **Mexico**.

Invite a **marionette** performer to visit the class and present a performance for the children.

Evaluation and Testing

1. Draw four **M** objects that you would like to give to your **mother** for **Mother's** Day.
2. Name a food that begins with the letter **M**.
3. Identify a printed **M**.
4. Give a girl's name that starts with an **M**.

Extra M Activities

Magic: Many children will be able to demonstrate simple **magic** tricks. Older students could be invited to show some **magic**. Two for starters might be:

1. Fill a bottle with water. Place a picture behind the bottle. When **moved**, the picture **magnifies** and **moves** the opposite way!
2. Loop a strip of paper into an "S" and clip the curves of the "S" with paper clips, as shown. Pull the ends and the clips fall off linked together!

Microscopes: If possible, obtain **microscopes** and slides for the children to view.

Manual Alphabet: Discuss problems that **mute** people have. Introduce the class to the alphabet that they use.

Magazines: Bring children's **magazines** for the class to look at. Have the children bring their own. Center activities around the **magazines**.

GA184

ZIP

Zz

ZOO

103

The Sound of the Week is "Z"

Timing

The sound of **Z** should be taught toward the end of the school year to supplement a **zoo** unit and an interest in spring and baby animals. Placement at the end of the year, when the children can build on experience with more common letters, is advantageous.

Special Environmental Considerations

Prepare a **zoo** mural background. If it is still available, the background for the "How It Goes?" mural (see **W** week) can be adapted by adding trees and shrubs. Included should be an area for the cats, a pool for seals and walrus, tall trees for giraffes, a monkey island, a pool for hippos, and rocks for bears. An area for a **zoo** of toy animals might be prepared as well so the children can bring their own and have experience in grouping and classifying the **zoo** families.

Whole Language, Reading and Math Readiness

Classification: Provide pictures or models of **zoo** animals for grouping and classification. **Zoo** animal crackers are good for this activity.

Zero: Discuss the concept of **zero** as a place holder. Indicate how it works in our number system based on 10. Emphasize that **zero** has other meanings besides nothing.

Language Arts Resources

Check the library for books, poems and films about **zoo, zero, zippers, zinnias, zip codes, zebras**.

Films:

Zero: Something for Nothing, Xerox Educational Corp.

Activities

Zoo Mural: Have the children paint and cut out pictures for the **zoo** mural.

Punch Dot Leopard: Duplicate an outline of a leopard no more than 6" wide. After the children cut out the leopard, they punch holes in it with a paper punch and the leopard is mounted on a black sheet of 9" × 12" construction paper. The black shows through the holes for the

GA184

leopard's spots.

Waggle Head Tiger: Prepare the two parts of a tiger as shown in the following illustrations.

Have the children color the stripes and features. Cut out the two parts, including a slot in the body for the head-tail parts. The tail is threaded through the slot and is used to wiggle the head. Have the children make tiger noises when playing with their animals.

Little Lion: (similar to Elephant, p. 83)
Fold 9″ × 12″ yellow paper twice to make a 6″ × 4½″ rectangle. Cut a half-circle from open edges. Clip a slot on fold to hold head. Cut a circle from a 4½″ square of brown and fringe around. Cut a circle from a 3″ yellow square. Assemble by putting yellow circle on fringed circle. Insert in clipped place on fold of body. Use half-circles cut from 9″ × 12″ for ears. Trim one to make a curved tail. Add a face (see side illustration).

Stand-Up Animals:

Fold a 9″ × 12″ sheet of construction paper. Cut an arch from the center of the open side. Cut a circle from a 6″ square for the head. The two pieces cut from the folded piece are used as ears for the elephant. A 1″ × 6″ strip of paper for a trunk will also be needed. Or, the two pieces cut from the folded paper can be used for a face and ears for the lion. The lion will also need a 6″ square cut in a circle and fringed for a mane (see side illustration).

GA184

Spool Animals: Prepare copies of both the front and back of animals. Have the children cut and glue the pieces to empty thread spools for stand-up animals (see illustrations).

Music

Records
Sesame Street Records has the song "Zizzy Zoomers." Also, Young People's Records has the song "Train to the Zoo."

Science, Health and Social Studies

Zinnias: Plant **zinnias** in containers. Plan to give them to a senior citizen or other friend the last week of school.

Snacks

Serve snacks such as **zoo** cookies (animal cookies), **zucchini, zucchini** bread and **zwieback** toast.

Special Fun

If there is a **zoo** in the area, make plans to visit.

Zoo cookie picture: Children can draw a **zoo** placemat and put crackers in the **zoo** before eating. Good classifying.

Evaluation and Testing

1. Draw four things that start with the letter **Z**.
2. Identify the letter **Z** in print.
3. Given pictures of three **zoo** animals, identify the one that starts with the letter **Z**.
4. Give a number that starts with the letter **Z**.

GA184

NO 9 nine Nn

107

The Sound of the Week is "N"

Timing

The sound of **N** is easy for children to grasp. It can be included anywhere in the program or during the month of **November**.

Special Environmental Considerations

Use affirming words such as **nice, neat** and **nifty** when responding to the children and different situations during the week.

Prepare word cards with the word **new** on them and attach them on **new** clothing and other **new** articles in the room throughout the week.

Whole Language, Reading and Math Readiness

News: Emphasize that show-and-tell this week can be on items of interest in the **news**. Discuss the various sources of **news**. Bring daily papers for reviewing **news** events once during the week. Develop a bulletin board of clippings that are brought in by the children. The clippings may be classified into different groups such as world, local, animal, sports, health, etc.

Near and Far: Provide opportunity for language and concept development by describing things that are **near** and far away.

Numbers: This is a good week to check on how the class as a whole is doing with mathematical objectives for the appropriate grade level. Skills such as counting, recognition of **numerals**, writing and grouping can be checked. Develop a plan for meeting the **needs** assessed.

Nickels: Provide coins for observation, counting and dramatic play.

Nine: Wherever appropriate, group and count in series of **nine**.

Language Arts Resources

Books:
Noisy Nancy Norris, LouAnn Gaeddert, Doubleday, 1965.
Nothing at All, Wanda Gag, Coward-McCann, 1941.
Nothing to Do, Russell Hoban, Harper, 1964.

GA184

Activities

Friendship Necklace: Give each child a duplicated page with a list of the children's **names** on it. Have the children cut out the **names** and string them into a **necklace**, using pieces of drinking straws, macaroni or packing foam for spacers.

Newsletter: Collect items of class **news**, plans, poems, creative writing, etc., and prepare a **newsletter** or **newspaper**. Determine the audience for the paper before publication.

Needle and Thread Pictures: Lengths of yarn threaded through darning or tapestry **needles** can be used to sew creative designs on Styrofoam meat trays.

Hammer and Nails: Encourage the children to bring hammers, assorted **nails** and scraps of wood from home. Hammer and **nail** activities can take several forms. For coordination development, an old log or stump can be used for pounding in **nails**. Pieces of wood and other materials can be **nailed** together into sculptures. The children can have fun **nailing** pieces of wood together to make "boats." (A carpet square under a child's work provides a good muffler of **noise** and at the same time protects the floor surface.)

Nurse Hats: Cut 8½" × 11" or 9" × 12" sheets of white paper into a "T" by cutting 3" squares from 2 corners. Fold back the long side. Add a cross if desired. Fasten the back to the corners (see sample).

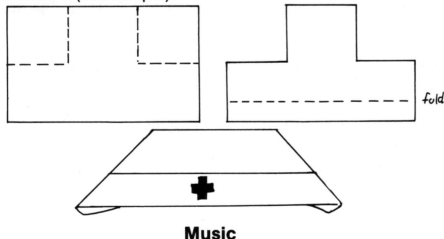

fold

Music

Songs:

"The North Wind" and "Nice Little Dog," from *Music for Young Americans* by Richard Berg, are just a couple of **N** letter songs.

Records: "Near and Far," "Noodle Song," "Nobody" and "People in Your Neighborhood" are songs that can be found on Sesame Street Records.

Special Note: Number and counting songs are excellent to use for this unit.

Science, Health and Social Studies

Nests: Collect and observe empty **nests**. Be sure to caution the children about **never** disturbing an occupied **nest**. List the building materials found in various **nests**. Try setting a **nest** in a pan of water. In a few days, the seeds in the grasses will sprout! Group and classify **nests** by size, location, materials used, etc. If possible, take the children on a walk to look for **nests**.

Noses: Observe and discuss characteristics, functions and special adaptations of various human and animal **noses**. Provide a variety of sniffing experiences.

Neighbors and Neighborhoods: Discuss and define these two **N** words. Focus on what makes a good **neighbor** or **neighborhood**.

Snacks

Serve the children **nuts, nougat, noodles** and **nut** bread. Or, serve the children **no** snack and discuss how it would feel to be without food. Invite children to bring **nuts** in shells and **nutcrackers**. Spend some time counting, sorting, and graphing—then cracking and eating.

Special Fun

Nurse: Arrange a visit with the school **nurse** or another **nurse**. In addition to sharing the job with the children, mention the discussion on **noses** and ask him/her to tell the children the function of the **nose** as a part of the body. He/She might also discuss the **neck** and **nails**.

Evaluation and Testing

1. Identify the upper and lower case letter **N** in print.
2. Draw pictures of **nine N** things.
3. **Name** two body parts that start with **N**.

red

GA184

The Sound of the Week is "R"

Timing

R week can be a filler wherever needed after the first few weeks of the program have been completed. Less mature children may have difficulty in hearing and pronouncing the **R** sound correctly. The letter **R** can be presented during spring with focus on **robins, rain** and **rocks**. Another possibility is to present this letter around Christmas and emphasize **reindeer**, especially **Rudolph**. If **reading readiness** tests are to be given, they might be done during **R** week.

Special Environmental Considerations

Letter **R** monograms should be cut out of **red** paper. Display pictures of **Rembrandt** and Norman **Rockwell** paintings. Use **R** expressions such as **right, right**-on and **really!** Use **red** pencil, paper, etc., as much as possible.

Whole Language, Reading and Math Readiness

Riddles: Collect, **read** or make up **riddles**.

Right and Left: If left and **right** activities were done during **L** week, the class may be **ready** for **review**. Otherwise, see **L** week for suggested activities.

Language Arts Resources

Books:

Clifford, the Big Red Dog, Norman Bridwell, Four Winds Press, 1973.

Rain Drop Splash, Alvin Tresselt, Lothrop, Lee & Shephard, 1946.

Red Is Never a Mouse, Eth Clifford, Bobbs-Merrill, 1960.

Restless Robin, Marjorie Flack, Houghton Mifflin, 1965.

Robins on the Windowsill, Irmengarde Eberle, Crowell, 1958.

Poetry:

"Recipe for a Hippopotamus Sandwich" can be found in Shel Silverstein's book *Where the Sidewalk Ends*.

My Rocks

On a cold and rainy day
When I can't get out to play,
I open up my treasure box
And look at all my pretty rocks.

GA184

I have rocks from here and there
I have rocks from everywhere.
Some are smooth, some are sandy
And there's one that looks like candy.

I have one that's shining clean
Another one that's blue and green.
All of them recall good times
Places I've been, hills I've climbed.

When the sun comes out to stay,
I'll put all my rocks away.
Close the lid and safely hide
All my treasures safe inside.　　　　Unknown

Radishes
We dig and rake
And plant and hoe.
We hope our radishes will grow.
But how, we wonder,
Will they know
That underneath a coat of red
They should be white
From toe to head
Inside the brown, dark
Garden bed?　　　　Unknown

Films:

Red Balloon, Macmillan Films.

Red Hen, Barr Films.

Robin Redbreast, Encyclopedia Britannica Educational Corp.

Rocks for Beginners, Modern Learning Aids.

Rumplestiltskin, Sterling Educational Films.

Activities

Raincoat Dolls: Trace the outline of a person, paper doll style, on a sheet of 12″ × 18″ paper. Prepare a folded coat and a simple hat to be cut and used to dress the doll. Note that the scraps from the coat become the umbrella and boots. The dolls display well against a background of newspaper, which tends to look like **rain** from a distance (see side illustration).

113

GA184

Red: Collect a variety of objects, materials and textures in **red**. Make **red** collages in box lids.

Robots: Ice cream barrels, oatmeal cartons, paper tubes, flexible tubing, foil, cellophane and pipe cleaners lend themselves to creating fantastic **robots**. The ice cream barrels alone make good helmets for dramatic play.

Recess: During **recess**, have the children play games such as **Red Rover**, jump **rope**, **Ring-A-Round-The-Roses**, **ring** toss, cops and **robbers**, **relay races** and a **reorganized** version of **rugby**.

Red: Have only **red** paint available one day. Also, play only with the **red** components of toys.

Music

Songs:
The music book *Music for Young Americans*, by Richard Berg, has the songs "Red Wagon," "Robin Song," "Roll That Red Ball" and "She'll Be Comin' 'Round the Mountain." *The Kindergarten Book*, by Lilla Belle Pitts, has the songs "Little Red Hen," "Ring-A-Round-The-Roses" and "Rock-A-Bye Baby."

Records:
The album *Learning Basic Skills Through Music, Vol. 1*, has the song "Colors." Sesame Street Records has the songs "The 'R' Machine" and "Rain Falls."

Rhythms:
Some possible **rhythms** could deal with **running, rolling** and a **rhythm** band.

Special Note: Play **records** with **ragtime** and **rock** 'n **roll**. Listen to music on the **radio**. Check sources for songs about **red, rain, robins**, and **rainbows**.

Science, Health and Social Studies

Rocks: Encourage the children to bring **rocks** to class. Have them observe and touch them. Then have the children classify the **rocks** in groups according to color, size, weight, **roughness** and smoothness.

GA184

Radishes: Plant **radishes** in a dishpan so that they will be **ready** to eat in approximately four weeks.

Running: This is a good time to check coordination skills to see how the children **run**. Speed is not so much a factor as body control and position. The children should **run** in an upright body position, with elbows bent, arms swinging (as opposed to being held out from the sides), and an even, **rhythmic** step. There is still not much extension of the legs (strides will be short).

Snacks

Dramatize the story of the Little **Red** Hen as a play. During the dramatization, make bread in class.

The children will also enjoy **Ritz** crackers, **Rice** Krispies, **Rye**-Krisp, **rock** candy, **radishes, raisins, roast** beef, **ravioli, raspberries, root** beer and having a wiener **roast**.

Special Fun

Red Day: Designate one day of the week as **Red** Day and encourage everyone to wear **red**. Sing **red** songs, **read** or see the film *Red Balloon* and have a **red** snack such as **red** Jell-O.

Red Cross: Ask a member of the **Red** Cross to visit the class and explain the organization's function.

Railroad Engineer: Invite a **railroad** engineer to visit the class and, through a vivid presentation, take the children on a train **ride**.

Roller-Skating Party: If possible, schedule a **roller**-skating party for the class. Or, if the children have some sidewalk **roller** skates, have them bring them to class for some **roller**-skating fun. This would be an excellent time to discuss **roller**-skating **rules** and safety.

Evaluation and Testing

1. Draw four things that are usually **red**.
2. Identify the upper case and lower case letter **R** in print.
3. Check each child's pronunciation of the letter **R**. Listen for the W sound as in "wabbit." Call the **R** sound the "**rooster**" sound and practice making it by going "r-r-r-r" in the cock-a-doodle-doo **rhythm**.

GA184

Extended R Activities

Rivers: Rivers are an important means of transportation. Discuss the use of barges, paddle wheels, sailboats, **rowboats** and motorboats. What are some things that are transported on the **river**? How about people, grain, lumber and coal?

116

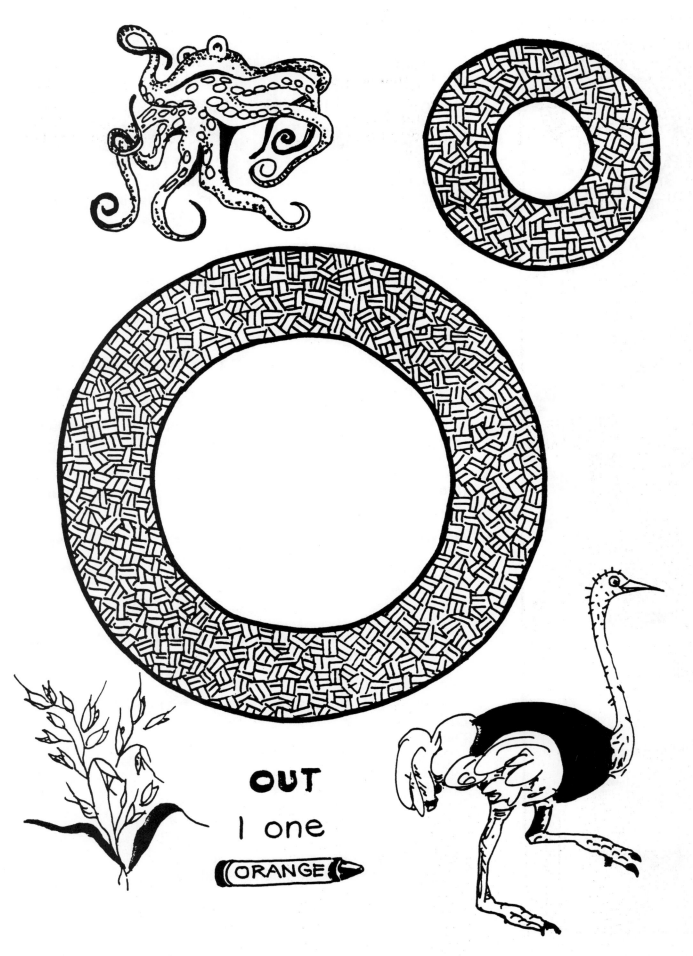

OUT

I one

ORANGE

GA184

The Sound of the Week is "O"

Timing

The **O** sound could be **one of** the last alphabet letters studied. Many primary reading teachers prefer to concentrate **on** vowel work when actual reading begins because **of** the phonic implications involved. Also, it may be convenient to deal with two letters in a single week. If this is not convenient, **O** can be presented in the month of **October**.

Special Environmental Considerations

Words like **one** and **orange** can be used as labels. The children could wear **orange** badges with the number 1 **on** them, indicating they are a Number **One** class. Use **orange** paper where practical.

Whole Language, Reading and Math Readiness

One: Develop the concept **of one** and more than **one**.

Old and New: Use the concept **of old** and new in language activities during this week.

Odd and Even: Discuss the concept **of odd** and even numbers with the children. Give them a few activities to accompany the discussion.

Opposites: Discuss the difference and usage of the words **off** and **on, open** and shut, **over** and under, etc.

Language Arts Resources

Obtain books, films and poems about **orange, owls, oceans, octopuses, ostriches**.

Books:
Orange Is a Color, Sharon Lerner, Lerner, 1970.
Open Your Eyes, Roz Abisch, Parents, 1964.
Owls, Herbert Zim, Morrow, 1950.

Poetry:
Check Shel Silverstein's book, *Where the Sidewalk Ends*, for **O** letter poems such as "**One** Inch Tall."

Films:
Ocean: A First Film, Bailey Film Associates.
Old Woman & Her Pig, McGraw-Hill Text Films.

Activities

Octopus: Children enjoy learning to braid in this activity. It involves attaching yarn **over** a ball **of** tissue **or** cotton,  dividing it into eight sections and braiding each **of** the sections (see illustration). This activity can lead to a discussion about the prefix **octo**-, meaning eight. Have **octagons** available for the children to **observe** and manipulate. They will enjoy playing with **other** words such as **octogenarian**.

Ornaments: Using beads, rickrack, string and glue, have the children decorate different sized Styrofoam balls. These **ornaments** can be stored and used to decorate Christmas trees. (Have the children donate the beads. Straight pins can also be used to hold the beads and rickrack, but the children must be carefully supervised.)

Orange: Have only **orange** paint available one day. Allow play with **only orange** components of toys.

Music

Songs:
The songs "Old MacDonald" and "Oh, Susanna" can be found in the song book *Music for Young Americans* by Richard Berg.

Records:
The movement song "Opposites" can be found on the album *Getting to Know Myself*, Educational Activities, Inc., Freeport, Long Island, New York. Sesame Street Records has the song "Would You Buy an O?"

Special Note: Check resources for counting songs using **one** and songs about **ostriches, octopuses, oceans, old,** etc.

Science, Health and Social Studies

Ostrich and Octopus: Obtain pictures, books, films, models and study prints for **observing** these "animals." Study their different habitats and compare them.

GA184

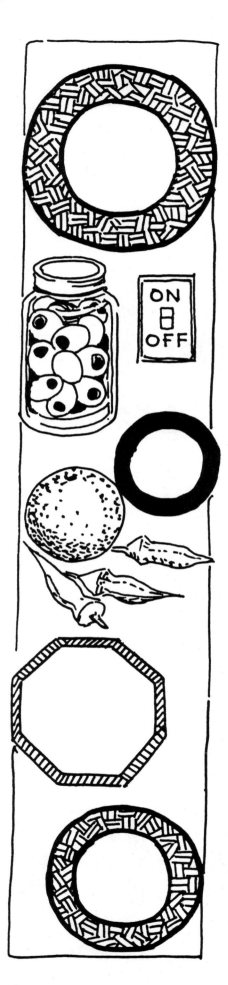

Maps: Display maps of **Ohio, Oklahoma** and **Oregon**. Mark significant sightseeing places for each state. Also, display pictures **of** the **Ozark** Mountains.

Olympics: Discuss the history **of** the **Olympics** and the different sports for **Olympic** participants.

Opossum: Display pictures **of opossums**. When they are trapped, they pretend to be dead. Explain what the term "playing possum" means.

Snacks

Oranges, oatmeal, Oreos, Oriental foods, **olives**, **okra**, and omelets are a few foods that can be served for snacks.

No Bake Orange Cookies

Mix in order:
   4 cups graham cracker crumbs (40 squares, crushed)
   1 cup powdered sugar
   ⅓ cup orange juice concentrate
   ¼ cup white Karo syrup
   ⅓ cup melted margarine
Add: nuts, raisins, oats, if desired. Form into balls about the size of walnuts. Roll in orange Jell-O powder. Let dry. Enjoy. Makes 4 dozen.

Special Fun

Listen to the school **orchestra**.
If possible, visit an **orchard**. Have a guide explain cultivation and techniques for growing the fruit.
Play records **of opera** and **organ** music.
Orange Day: Have children wear **orange**, bring **orange** things to share, and eat an **orange** snack.

Evaluation and Testing

1. Draw four things that start with the letter **O**.
2. Identify an **O** in print.

Extra O Activities

O'Clock: Have the children practice telling time.

Oriental Display: Create an **Oriental** display. This might include jade designs, **Oriental** rugs and material, and a discussion of the **Oriental** people.

GA184

I in

The Sound of the Week is "I"

Timing

Like **O**, the children hear the sound of **I** easily and learn **it in** a few days. **It** can be dealt with near the end of the program, or centered around Thanksgiving, when study can be placed on **Indians**.

Special Environmental Considerations

Provide a place for a display of **Indian items**.

Prepare a place to classify long and short **I** sounds.

Whole Language, Reading and Math Readiness

Ice Cream: Record and graph favorite flavors.

In and Out: Language development can focus on these two terms. Make labels and attach them to appropriate **items in** the classroom and environment.

Inches: Prepare a paper with lines of various lengths. Have children measure lines with rulers or cubes. Discuss the terms **inch**, foot, and yard. How many **inches** are in a foot? a yard?

In the Box, Out of the Box Game: Listening skills can be developed with this variation of the old "Simon Says" game. The leader calls out "Jack-**In**-The Box" or "Jack -Out-Of-The-Box" and the children respond by crouching or jumping up. They are not to change positions on the commands "**In**-The-Box" or "Out-Of-The-Box," but are to wait for Jack to tell them what to do. The object **is** to see who can go the longest without making a mistake.

Language Arts Resources

Check sources for books, films, and poems about **Indians, insects, inches, ice, ice cream**.

Books:
Indian Two Feet and His Horse, Margaret Friskey, Children's Press, 1971.
Inside, Outside, Upsidedown, Stan Berenstain, Random, 1968.
Ira Sleeps Over, Bernard Waber, Houghton-Mifflin, 1972.

Poetry:
Check Shel Silverstein's book *Where the Sidewalk Ends* for **I** poems such as "One Inch Tall."

GA184

Activities

Indian Headbands: Have the children fold a 4″ × 24″ strip of construction paper and **insert** real or paper feathers. Provide examples of **Indian** symbols for decoration.

Indian Beads: A variety of materials can be **incorporated into** necklaces. Shells, pieces of Styrofoam packing material, Cheerios, macaroni, beads and cut-up drinking straws are just a few.

Indian Shirts: By cutting neck and arm openings and making a slash up the front of it, a large grocery sack can be made **into** a simple but effective shirt. Don't forget the fringe at the bottom and decorations of beads, painting or coloring.

Iris: Each child needs a 6″ square of paper. Fold this into fourths. Hold the folded corner and cut to round off the other three corners, still leaving the paper intact. The result **is** a four-petaled shape. To form an **iris**, bring up two opposite petals and paste them. Curl the other pair downward. Attach a sturdy stem.

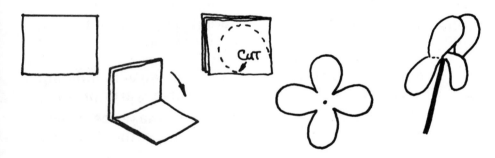

Music

Records:
There are several **I** letter songs that can be found on albums. Sesame Street Records has the songs "Everyone Likes Ice Cream" and "Indian Rhythms." Young People's Records has the song "Little Indian Drum."

Special Note: Check sources for songs about **Indians, insects, ice, igloos, inchworms, Independence** Day and **I**.

GA184

Science, Health and Social Studies

Indians: There are many areas of **Indian** culture that are of **interest** to small children. Whatever areas are developed, an effort should be made to emphasize the similarities to the culture with which the children are familiar and the positive contributions of **Indians** to today's culture, and to debunk the negative myths which have come out of the commercial media.

Ice: Provide opportunities to experiment and observe water as a solid. How **is ice** used? One way **is** for **ice** skating. Another way **is** for playing hockey.

Invisible Ink Messages: Write a message to each child using lemon juice and a cotton swab. Let it dry. The message can be revealed by an adult pressing it with a hot iron for the child to read.

Snacks

Iced tea, **Italian** foods, **instant** foods and icing are a few possibilities for snacks.

Impossible Pie: Mix together:

½ cup all-purpose baking mix	2 cups milk
1 cup sugar	1 teaspoon vanilla
4 eggs	add ½ cup coconut,
½ teaspoon salt	if desired

Pour **into** ungreased 10-**inch** pie pan. Sprinkle with nutmeg. Bake at 350 degrees for 55 minutes. Serve warm or cold.

Ice Cream: For a fun celebration plan to make **ice** cream **in** school. Ask parents to lend and operate the freezers. Or . . . make **individual** freezers that will serve 2 or 3 each. Fill a small coffee can ½ full with ice cream base. Tape the lid all around. Put the small can **inside** a large can; add rock salt and crushed **ice** (about 3 parts **ice** to 1 part rock salt) **in** alternating layers until the space between the cans **is** full. Tape the lid all around. Children shake or roll the can for about 20 minutes. Eat and enjoy!

Evaluation and Testing

1. Name four things that start with the letter **I**.
2. Give a word containing a long **I** and then one containing a short **I**.
3. **Identify** the upper and lower case letter **I in** print.
4. Measure a line **in inches**.

124

The Sound of the Week is "Q"

Timing

The letter **Q** is often more difficult for the children to grasp. Since **Q** always needs **U**, it is practical to deal with both **Q** and **U** simultaneously. It might be better to teach this letter late in the program. Refer all week to things that can be done **quickly**.

Special Environmental Considerations

Set aside areas of the bulletin board for both **Q** and **U**, if they are combined for study, so there is no chance of confusing the two sounds and letters.

Whole Language, Reading and Math Readiness

Quitting: Discuss advantages (safety) and disadvantages (learning) of **quitting**.

Questions: Discuss and give experience in asking and answering **questions**. Give opportunity to differentiate between other kinds of statements and **questions**. Give answers and have the children make up **questions** that would elicit the given answers.

Quart and Quarter: Discuss the terms **quarter** and **quart** with the children. How many **quarts** in a gallon? How many **quarters** in a dollar? Bring as many examples of **quarts** as possible.

Question Mark: There are several forms of punctuation. Show the different punctuation marks, but emphasize the use of a **question** mark after a **question**.

Language Arts Resources

Books:
How Big Is a Foot? (Queen), Rolf Myller, Atheneum, 1962.
Question and Answer Book About Nature, John Saunders, Random House, 1962.
Quiet on Account of Dinosaur, Jane Thayer, Morrow, 1964.
Quiet Mother and the Noisy Little Boy, Charlotte Zolotow, Lothrop, 1953.

GA184

Drama:
Develop an informal skit of a fairy tale that has a **queen** in it. Give everyone a chance to dress up and play the part.

Activities

Quilting: This experience can take one of many forms, from the simplest to the most complex, depending on the interest and skill of the teacher. The children could simply draw a pattern on a plain piece of quilted fabric, using permanent markers, stitch it to a bed pad or other filler, and tie knots with yarn. Each child could make an individual square or bring a patch of fabric used to make something at home. This can be assembled into a patchwork **quilt** that would be hand tied after assembly. Patches depicting events of the school year could be drawn with indelible felt pens and made into a **quilt** to be passed on to the doll corner for next year's class.

Music

Records:
The songs "Q" and "Question Song" can be found on Sesame Street Records.

Special Note: Try to find songs about ducks (**quack, quack**), **Quakers, quail** and Don **Quixote**.

This would be a good time to introduce musical terms such as **quarter** note, **quarter** rest and **quartet**.

Science, Health and Social Studies

Queen Bee: Discuss the role of the **queen** bee. Why is she important to the bee hive? What are the important jobs of the **queen** bee?

Queens: Discuss and explore the concept of **queens** and both fairy tale and real life **queens** of countries today. Try to define the concept with the children. Discuss why the United States could not have a **queen**.

Quick: Perform many activities to show that **quick** is not an absolute speed but must have something to compare.

Snacks

Quince jelly, **quiche, quail** and **quick** breads are a few snacks that can be served to the children. Cut snacks into **quarters**.

GA184

Impossible Quiche

Mix together:
- 1½ cup milk
- 3 eggs
- ½ cup melted butter (or margarine)
- ½ cup all-purpose baking mix
- ¼ teaspoon salt and pepper

Add 1 cup grated cheese, ½ cup chopped ham, bacon, onion, green pepper or mushrooms.

Pour into buttered pie pan. Bake at 350 degrees for 45 minutes, until set.

Special Fun

If your area has a pageant and a ruling **queen**, see if she would be available to visit. Direct discussions toward the concept that **queens** are real people. Queen For The Day: Any girls have a birthday this week? Name that child **Queen For The Day** and crown her. Or, let several girls be **queens** each day so each gets a turn during the week.

Invite a **quartet** from the school choir or band to visit the class and sing or play a few songs for the children.

Evaluation and Testing

1. Name four words that start with the letter **Q**.
2. Name the letter that **Q** always needs in every word.
3. Identify the upper and lower case letter **Q** in print.

Extra Q Activities

Quilt Show: Invite students to bring quilts to class. Allow time to tell about them. Display them by spreading them on tables and even the floor. Allow children to remove shoes and sit on them. Be sure to be careful of old or fragile **quilts**.

GA184

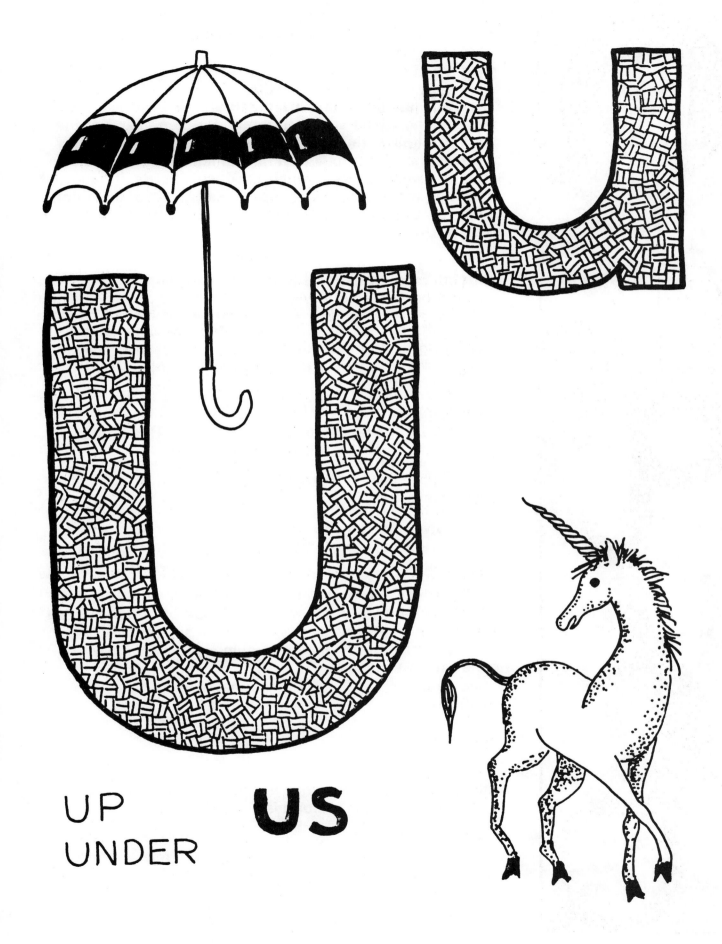

UP
UNDER

US

129

The Sound of the Week is "U"

Timing

Like other less commonly **used** letters, **U** is best dealt with near the end of the sound program. By then, many of the children already recognize it. Since there are not many activities that relate to **U** as an initial sound, and since the letter **Q** always needs **U** when **used** with words, it can be combined with **Q** for student identification. Also, the letter **U** can be presented in October near the time of trick or treat for **UNICEF**.

Special Environmental Considerations

Be prepared to deal with the long and short sounds of **U**. Group different examples on a divided board or table as either long or short **U**. Another space might be provided for **Q** words and labels to show that the letter **U** always follows **Q** in print.

Whole Language, Reading and Math Readiness

Up and Down: Prepare **up** label cards and identify things that are **up**. Play an "**up**-and down" variation of the game "Simon Says."

Under: Give some time to the concept of **under**. Again, word cards can add meaning to the concept and to the recognition of the letter **U**.

Un: Introduce the prefix **un** to the children. Explain that **un** in front of a word can mean *not, lack of, the opposite of,* or *the reverse* or *removal of.* Give them different **un** words and have them figure out their meanings. Some of the words in the list could include:

unarmed	unaware
unbearable	unbutton
undemanding	undeserving
unequal	unreachable
unsure	unuseable

Uniforms: List as many kinds as the class can think of. Try to determine why the **uniform** is needed or worn.

U Abbreviations: Explain the term *abbreviating* to the children, and how abbreviations are **used**. A few words that might be considered are:

GA184

UNICEF	**United** Nations International Children's Emergency Fund
U.S.A.	**United** States of America
U.S.A.F.	**United** States Air Force
U.S.M.C.	**United** States Marine Corps
U.S.O.	**United** Service Organization

Uncle: Talk about **uncles**, how one becomes an **uncle**, and whether any of the students (or teacher) are **uncles**. Talk about things children have done with **uncles**.

Language Arts Resources

Books:
Ugly Duckling, Hans Christian Andersen, Houghton, 1965.
Umbrella, Tara Yashima, Viking, 1958.
Uncle Sam's 200th Birthday Parade, Irwin Shapiro, Golden, 1974.
Unhappy Hippopotamus, Nancy Moore, Vanguard, 1957.
Unhappy Rabbit, Nancy Raymond, Fidler, 1955.

Poetry:

The Walking "U"
I have a **U** that opens so high
I think my **U** is bigger than I.
Whenever it's raining I walk down the street
And all people see are my two little feet.
I have to peek over or under the brim
To see where I'm going and where I have been
So if you are out in the rain you will see
A walking **U** and under it's me!

Unknown

Special Note: Shel Silverstein's book *Where the Sidewalk Ends* has the poems "Unicorn," "Upstairs" and "Us."

Films:
Understanding Fire, Coronet Films.
Ugly Duckling, Coronet Films.

Activities

Umbrella: Take an 8″ × 12″ piece of paper and fold it into fourths. Now, instead of leaving the edges squared, take scissors and round them off. There should be a circle when you open the paper. The circle should be divided into four sections. Use scissors to cut the folded line (leave attached in center). Now overlap the cut edges to make the circle into an **umbrella** top. Paste the pieces together in their overlapped position. Use scissors to scallop the edge. Next, take a straw and glue it to the inside center of the **umbrella**. Decorate the umbrella. The poem, "The Walking **U**" in the poetry section can accompany this activity.

GA184

Umbrella Picture: An effective **umbrella** picture can be made to accompany the "Walking **U**" poem by scalloping a half-circle on which the poem has been printed and pasting it on a piece of newspaper (classifieds are best) that has been spattered with a blue wash to look like raindrops. Add boots below and a few puddles.

Music

Songs:
"Under My Umbrella" can be found in the song book *The Kindergarten Book*, by Lilla Belle Pitts.

Records:
Sesame Street Records has the songs "The Letter U" and "Your Rich Uncle Died."

Special Note: Try to find records with **ukelele** music and play them for the children.

Science, Health and Social Studies

United States: Through maps and discussion, begin to develop a concept of the **United** States both in size and **unity**.

Urban and Rural: Center a discussion around the similarities and differences of **urban** and rural living. Discuss the locations of both and the different lifestyles.

Snacks

Serve the children a special treat! Fix **upside**-down cake for a snack.

Special Fun

If possible, invite a **unicyclist** to visit the class. Maybe he/she can perform for the students.

See if a band member or parent knows how to play the **ukelele**. If so, ask that person to come play for the class.

Evaluation and Testing

1. Name four things that start with the letter **U**.
2. Name two directions that start with the letter **U**.
3. Identify the **upper** and lower case letter **U** in print.

yes

yellow

GA184

The Sound of the Week is "Y"

Timing

Since it is less commonly used as an initial sound, combine the letter **Y** with another of the less common letters such as **X** or **Z** to present near the end of the program.

Special Environmental Considerations

Use as much **yellow** color as possible this week for monograms and labels. Respond to the children as often as possible with the word **yes**. Especially emphasize the verbal response rather than the non-verbal response of head shakes. Display pictures of **Yosemite** National Park, **Yellowstone** National Park, and the **Yukon** throughout the room. Also display a map of **Yugoslovia**.

Whole Language, Reading and Math Readiness

Yes and Yellow: These words should become sight words for most of the children during the week. Ask the children **Yes**, No questions. Have them point out different objects that have the color **yellow**. Use **yellow** paper wherever possible.

The Letter Y: Discuss with the children how the letter **Y** is used as both a vowel and a consonant. Show them examples of each. The following words can be used.

yacht	lightly
yard	gypsy
year	hyphen
yoke	python
yucca	syrup

Language Arts Resources

Books:

Big Yellow Balloon, Edward Fenton, Doubleday, 1967.
Year Without a Santa Claus, Phyllis McGinley, Lippincott, 1957.
Yertle the Turtle, Dr. Seuss, Random House, 1950.
You and Your Senses, Leo Schreider, Harcourt, 1956.

Activities

Yarn Pictures: This activity can take two forms. Either pictures can be drawn with white glue and yarn applied for color, or darning needles threaded with **yarn** can be used to make stitching on Styrofoam meat trays. If the use of needles is chosen, make sure the children are well supervised.

GA184

Yellow: Have the children collect **yellow** objects for a collage. The collages can be made individually with articles glued in meat trays or made in groups. Have only **yellow** paint and allow only **yellow** components of toys for play one day.

Yelling: Center a discussion around **yelling**. Why do people **yell**? Do **you yell**? Why? What are some **Y yelling** words? Some words that can be used are **yeah, yahoo, yippee** and **yoo-hoo**.

Young and Old: Have the children list the characteristics of **young** and old people. Are there similarities and differences? What are they?

Music

Songs:
One possible **Y** letter song that children enjoy is "Yankee Doodle."

Records:
Sesame Street Records has the song "Your Rich Uncle Died."

Find songs with **yodeling**. The song "The Lonely Goat Herd," from the movie *The Sound of Music*, is a **yodeling** song. Let the children practice **yodeling**.

Special Note: Check song book indexes for songs with the subject of **yards, yams, yes, yeoman** and **yesterday**.

Science, Health and Social Studies

Yellow: Yellow is a color in nature. Look for and collect specimens of **yellow** from nature. Classify the specimens into different categories such as animal, vegetable and mineral. Try to determine why some things in nature are **yellow**—for camouflage, attractions, minerals, etc.

Mr. Yuk: Review poison control information learned during **P** week. Distribute Mr. **Yuk** stickers available free from local Poison Control Centers. Explain to the children why Mr. **Yuk** is found on many bottles.

Yesterday: Be sure everyone in class understands the concept and meaning of the term **yesterday**. Provide experiences to demonstrate this awareness if some are uncertain.

 GA184

Snacks

Serve the children **yummy** snacks such as **yams, yogurt, yellow** cake, **yeast** rolls and bread.

Special Fun

Visit a **YMCA** or a **YWCA**. Or, invite someone from one of the organizations to visit the class. Have them discuss different activities scheduled for children at the **Y**.

Evaluation and Testing

1. Name four objects that are **yellow**.
2. Name four words that start with the letter **Y**.
3. Identify **yes** and **yellow** in print.
4. Tell something **you** did **yesterday**.

Extra Y Activities

Yellow Day: Have children wear **yellow** and bring **yellow** things to share. Have a **yellow** snack.

Yellow means caution. Have pictures in the room of the different road signs. Show the children distinguishing characteristics of each sign. Some signs that might be used are the **yield** sign, stop sign, railroad sign, no passing sign and pass with care sign.

GA184

CROSS STITCH

X-RAY

137

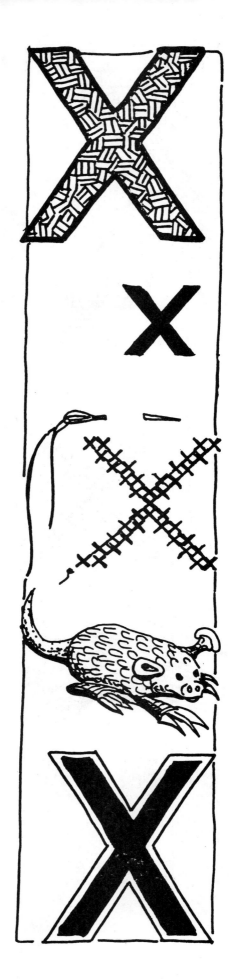

The Sound of the Week is "X"

Timing

Combine the study of the letter **X** with another of the less commonly used letters near the end of the program.

Special Environmental Considerations

Be prepared to explain that many words which sound like they start with **X** really start with the letter **E** and have **X** for the second letter. Practice saying the **EX** words such as **extra, exact, example, exercise, exist,** and **explore.** Help the children see how the **Eh** sound comes first. During the week accept **EX** words by placing them on a separate bulletin board from words that really start with the letter **X**.

Language Arts Resources

Books:
X Marks the Spot, Marilyn Hafner, Coward, 1972.

Poetry:

> **X** in the Roman notation is ten,
> **X** is the mark of illiterate men;
>
> **X** means a crossing, as drivers may note,
> **X** in a square also counts as a vote;
>
> **X** is a quantity wholly unknown,
> **X** is a ruler removed from his throne;
>
> **X**mas is Christmas, a season of bliss,
> **X** in a letter is good for one kiss;
>
> **X** is for Xerxes, a monarch renowned,
> **X** marks the spot where treasure is found;
>
> Fickle as air or the capricious hex
> What a truly remarkable letter is **X**.
>
> Anonymous

(Explain these different meanings to the children.)

Activity

Cross-Stitch: Some children will enjoy being shown how to cross-stitch with yarn in meat trays or on 1" graph paper. Others will want to make designs by drawing crosses on graph paper. Show samples of old samplers and other items that have been cross-stitched. The children might also enjoy seeing other types of embroidery stitches.

Music

Records:
One **X** letter song that can be found on Sesame Street Records is "X Marks the Spot."

Science, Health and Social Studies

X-Rays: If given plenty of notice, many doctors and dentists are willing to supply **x**-rays which they would otherwise discard. Try to obtain old **x**-ray film of major bones and teeth. Hang them in the windows for the children to look at. It is interesting to compare an **x**-ray of a broken bone with that of a healthy one. Show the children **x**-rays of teeth with dental caries. Compare teeth with cavities and teeth without. Also show the children **x**-rays of baby teeth with the permanent teeth waiting below the gum line.

Snacks

Hot Cross buns could be served. But, whatever snack is chosen, make enough so that the children can have **x**-tra helpings.

Special Fun

X-ray Technician: If possible, have an **x**-ray technician visit and show the **x**-rays described in the Science, Health and Social Studies Section.

Treasure Hunt: This makes a good last-day-of-school activity. Arrange a treasure hunt around the school yard. Have the "treasure" in a box marked with an **X**. The treasure might be an "Alphabet Salad" which uses ingredients from all the letters of the alphabet.

Alphabet Salad

Mix together:
Apples
Bananas
Cherries
Dates
(don't **E**at yet)
Figs
Grapefruit (or **G**rapes)
Honey

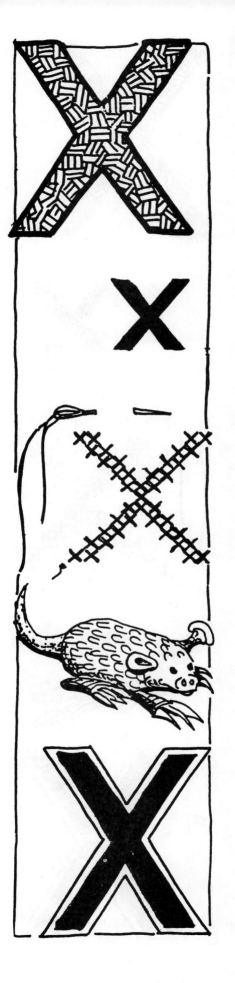

GA184

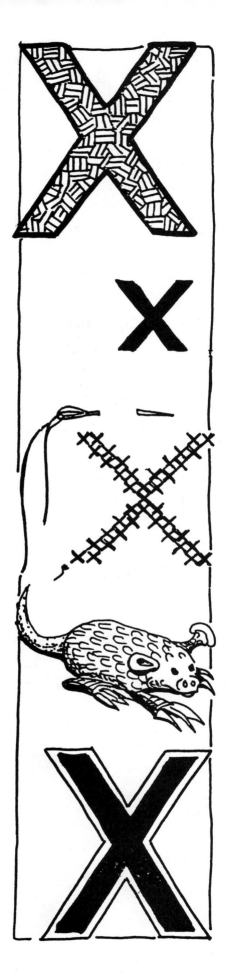

Ice Cream
Juice
Kumquats
Lemon
Marshmallows
Nuts
Oranges
Pineapple
Quince Jelly
Raspberries (or Raisins)
Strawberries
Tangerines
Use Utensils
Vanilla
Watermelon
(for X-tra flavor)
Yogurt
(eat with Zest!)

If possible, have a band member visit the class and give a performance playing the **xylophone**. Maybe the children have toy **xylophones** at home. Have the children bring them to class and have their own concert performances.

Evaluation and Testing

1. Name two objects that start with the letter **X**.
2. Name two things that **X** stands for.
3. Identify the letter **X** in print.
4. Have the children make a cross-stitch design.
5. Differentiate between **X** and **EX** words. Give examples of each.

GA184

Appendix

Books

Beattle, John and others, *The American Singer, Book I.* New York: American Book Co., 1944.

Berg, Richard and others. *Music For Young Americans.* New York: American Book Co., 1959.

Dalton, Alene and others. *My Picture Book Of Songs.* New York: M.A. Donahue, 1947.

Nielsen, Patricia and others. *Mockingbird Flight.* Indianapolis: The Economy Co., 1975.

Pitts, Lilla Belle and others. *The Kindergarten Book.* New York: Ginn & Co., 1959.

Related Books

Coleman, Satis. *Another Singing Time.* New York: John Day Co., 1946.

_____. *Singing Time.* New York: John Day Co., 1946.

Jaye, Mary T., and Imogene Hilyard. *Making Music Your Own.* Atlanta: Silver Burdette Co., 1966.

Neidlinger, W. H. *Small Songs For Small Singers.* New York: G. Schirmer, 1907.

Walters, Lorrain and others. *The Magic Of Music—Kindergarten.* Boston: Ginn & Co., 1970.

Records

Activity Records, Educational Activities, Inc., Freeport, Long Island, New York

Learning Basic Skills Through Music, Vol. 1
Learning Basic Skills Through Music, Vol. 2
Getting To Know Myself

Phoebe James Productions, Box 134, Pacific Palisades, California

Young People Records—Children's Record Guild, 100 6th Avenue, New York, 13, New York

Sesame Street Records, Children's Television Workshop, 159 W. 53rd Street, New York, New York

Bert's Blockbusters
The Electric Company
Letters and Numbers
Pete Seeger And Brothers Kirk
    Visit Sesame Street
Sing the Hit Songs of Sesame Street

Let A Frown Be Your Umbrella
People In Your Neighborhood
C is for Cookie
Ernie's Hits
Big Bird Sings

GA184

THE GROWING FAMILY OF GOOD ⊕ APPLE PRODUCTS AND SERVICES INCLUDES:

5 Periodicals to Meet the Needs of Educators

THE GOOD APPLE NEWSPAPER For grades 2-8. Each issue contains BIG (17½ x 22½) pages filled with creative, easy-to-use ideas. Features include full-size gameboards, seasonal units, reproducible activity pages, and much more. A wealth of ideas coming your way five times each year.

LOLLIPOPS For preschool-grade 2. Each issue provides timely teaching tips and professional articles that help to create a happy classroom environment. A special section of tear-out reproducible activity sheets and special units accompany this popular periodical. *Lollipops* comes your way five times each school year.

CHALLENGE Reaching and teaching the gifted child k-8. Each exciting issue contains a section of easy-to-use, practical and motivating activities. Other features include complete units of study, tips for parents of gifted children, interviews with gifted adults and children and much more. *Challenge* comes your way five times each school year.

OASIS For grades 5-9. *Oasis* contains reproducible activity sheets for all content areas, articles on the most current topics, interdisciplinary units plus much more. *Oasis* is published five times each school year to provide you with a continuous flow of new and exciting ideas.

SHINING STAR An exciting Christian education publication for k-8. Each issue includes motivating ideas, bulletin boards, Bible games, crafts, seasonal activities, reproducible work sheets and more. For use in church, home and school. *Shining Star* is published quarterly.

Good Apple Idea and Activity Books

In all subject areas for all grade levels, preschool-12. Idea books, activity books, bulletin board books, units of instruction, reading, creativity, readiness, gameboards, science, math, social studies, responsibility education, self-concept, gifted, seasonal ideas, arts/crafts, poetry, language arts, and teacher helpers.

Good Apple has just the book you have been looking for

and

Activity Posters • Note Pads • Software • Videos

and there is still more!

Good Apple is also proud to distribute Monday Morning Books. This fine line of educational products includes creativity, arts and crafts, reading, language arts and early learning resources.

Shining Star is a division of Good Apple, Inc. Its products include Christian education material for school, church and home. For grades k-8.

Workshops

Good Apple can provide your school with the workshop to meet your needs. We have a variety of specialists who will design the workshop specifically for your school.

If a school supply store is not available in your area, please write for a FREE catalog to Good Apple, Inc., Box 299, Carthage, IL 62321-0299